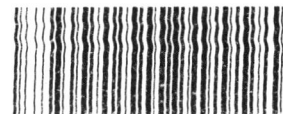

CAMBRIDGE
UNIVERSITY PRESS

CAMBRIDGE
Primary Science

Teacher's Resource 6

Fiona Baxter & Liz Dilley

CAMBRIDGE
UNIVERSITY PRESS

University Printing House, Cambridge CB2 8BS, United Kingdom

One Liberty Plaza, 20th Floor, New York, NY 10006, USA

477 Williamstown Road, Port Melbourne, VIC 3207, Australia

314–321, 3rd Floor, Plot 3, Splendor Forum, Jasola District Centre, New Delhi – 110025, India

103 Penang Road, #05–06/07, Visioncrest Commercial, Singapore 238467

Cambridge University Press is part of the University of Cambridge.

It furthers the University's mission by disseminating knowledge in the pursuit of education, learning and research at the highest international levels of excellence.

www.cambridge.org
Information on this title: www.cambridge.org/9781108785365

© Cambridge University Press 2021

Cambridge International copyright material in this publication is reproduced under licence and remains the intellectual property of Cambridge Assessment International Education.

First published 2014
Second edition 2021

20 19 18 17 16 15 14 13 12 11 10 9 8 7 6 5 4 3 2

Printed in Great Britain by CPI Group (UK) Ltd, Croydon CR0 4YY

A catalogue record for this publication is available from the British Library

ISBN 9781108785365 Paperback with Digital access

> Contents

Teaching notes

Digital resources

The following items are available on Cambridge GO. For more information on how to access and use your digital resource, please see inside front cover.

Active learning

Assessment for Learning

Developing learner language skills

Differentiation

Improving learning through questioning

Language awareness

Metacognition

Skills for Life

Letter for parents – Introducing the Cambridge Primary resources

Lesson plan template and examples of completed lesson plans

Curriculum framework correlation

Scheme of work

Diagnostic check and answers

Mid-year test and answers

End-of-year test and answers

Answers to Learner's Book questions

Answers to Workbook questions

Glossary

You can download the following resources for each unit:

Differentiated worksheets and answers

Language worksheets and answers

Resource sheets

End-of-unit tests and answers

⟩ Acknowledgements

The authors and publishers acknowledge the following sources of copyright material and are grateful for the permissions granted. While every effort has been made, it has not always been possible to identify the sources of all the material used, or to trace all copyright holders. If any omissions are brought to our notice, we will be happy to include the appropriate acknowledgements on reprinting.

Thanks to the following for permission to reproduce images:

Cover image by Omar Aranda (Beehive Illustration)

Inside Teacher Book LP7/GI; Fran Garca/GI

In Worksheets Xuanyu Han/GI; majorosl/GI; In Tests R.Tsubin/GI; sakdinon/GI; desertsolitaire/GI; R.Tsubin/GI; Pawel Toczynski/GI

Key: GI= Getty Images

> Introduction

Welcome to the new edition of our Cambridge Primary Science series.

Since its launch, the series has been used by teachers and learners in over 100 countries for teaching the Cambridge Primary Science curriculum framework.

This exciting new edition has been designed by talking to Primary Science teachers all over the world. We have worked hard to understand your needs and challenges, and then carefully designed and tested the best ways of meeting them.

As a result of this research, we've made some important changes to the series. This Teacher's Resource has been carefully redesigned to make it easier for you to plan and teach the course.

The series still has extensive digital and online support, including Digital Classroom, which lets you share books with your class and play videos and audio. This Teacher's Resource also offers extra teaching guidance and downloadable resources.

The series uses the most successful teaching pedagogies like active learning and metacognition, and this Teacher's Resource gives you full guidance on how to integrate them into your classroom.

Formative assessment opportunities help you to get to know your learners better, with clear learning objectives and success criteria as well as an array of assessment techniques, including advice on self and peer assessment.

Clear, consistent differentiation ensures that all learners are able to progress in the course with tiered activities, differentiated worksheets and advice about supporting learners' different needs.

All our resources are written for teachers and learners who use English as a second or additional language. They help learners build core English skills with vocabulary and grammar support, as well as additional language worksheets.

We hope you enjoy using this course.

Eddie Rippeth

Head of Primary and Lower Secondary Publishing, Cambridge University Press

> About the authors

Fiona Baxter

Fiona Baxter has been involved in Science education for over 25 years and has many years of Science teaching experience. In recent years her main focus has been on developing learning materials for both primary and secondary school curricula. One of Fiona's areas of interest in Science education is making science more accessible to both teachers and learners, particularly in developing countries, through the use of low cost, everyday materials for practical work. She also feels strongly about the inclusion of girls in Science activities in the classroom and the workplace.

Fiona believes that using the Cambridge Primary Science series will help learners to build a strong conceptual foundation for further studies in Science, while at the same time making the learning experience engaging and fun.

Liz Dilley

Liz was born and educated in London and did a BSc and post graduate diploma in Education at the University of Bristol.

Shortly after university she moved to South Africa, where she taught for several years before training as a second-language English writer. This led to a variety of experiences in teacher training, adult education and writing for school-aged learners.

From the mid-1990s Liz began to focus more on writing textbooks for Life Sciences, Physical Science and Social Sciences. She wrote textbooks for the new Namibian curriculum and later the new South African curriculum – about 200 titles in total.

In 2012–2016 she co-authored the Cambridge Primary Science Series and is now a co-author of the new series.

Liz lives in Cape Town, South Africa, with her husband and family. She enjoys hiking, boating and travelling to interesting places.

> How to use this series

All of the components in the series are designed to work together.

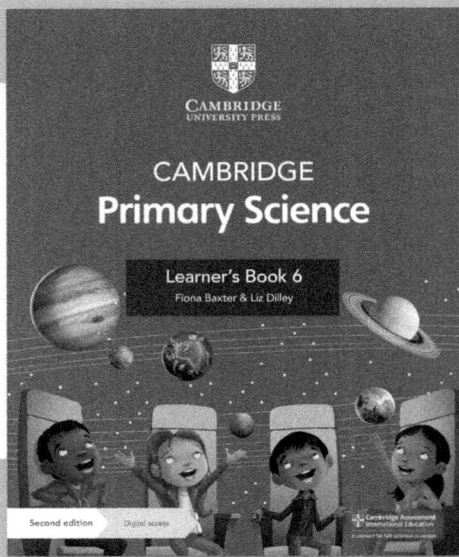

The Learner's Book is designed for learners to use in class with guidance from the teacher. It offers complete coverage of the curriculum framework. A variety of investigations, activities, questions and images motivate students and help them to develop the necessary scientific skills. Each unit contains opportunities for formative assessment, differentiation and reflection so you can support your learners' needs and help them progress.

The Teacher's Resource is the foundation of this series and you'll find everything you need to deliver the course in here, including suggestions for differentiation, formative assessment and language support, teaching ideas, answers, tests and extra worksheets. Each Teacher's Resource includes:

- A **print book** with detailed teaching notes for each topic

- **Digital Access** with all the material from the book in digital form plus editable planning documents, extra guidance, worksheets and more.

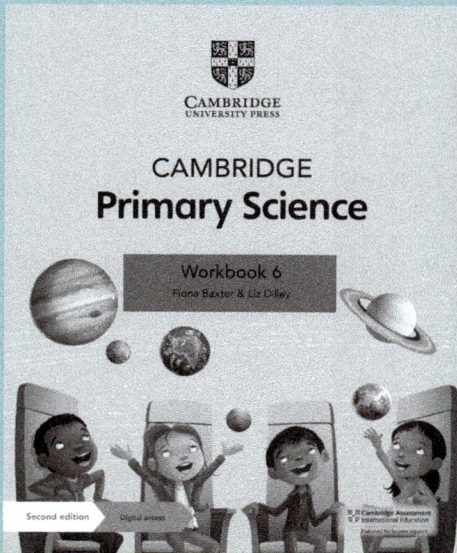

The skills-focused write-in Workbook provides further practice of all the topics in the Learner's Book and is ideal for use in class or as homework. A three-tier, scaffolded approach to skills development promotes visible progress and enables independent learning, ensuring that every learner is supported. Teachers can assign learners questions from one or more tiers for each exercise, or learners can progress through each of the tiers in the exercise.

Digital Classroom includes digital versions of the Learner's Book and Workbook, complete with pop-up answers, designed for teachers to use at the front of class. Easily share the books with the whole class on your whiteboard, zoom in, highlight and annotate text, and get your learners talking with videos, images and interactive activities.

A letter to parents, explaining the course, is available to download from Cambridge GO (as part of this Teacher's Resource).

> How to use this Teacher's Resource

This Teacher's Resource contains both general guidance and teaching notes that help you to deliver the content in our Cambridge Primary Science resources. Some of the material is provided as downloadable files, available on **Cambridge GO**. (For more information about how to access and use your digital resource, please see inside front cover.) See the Contents page for details of all the material available to you, both in this book and through Cambridge GO.

Teaching notes

This book provides **teaching notes** for each unit of the Learner's Book and Workbook. Each set of teaching notes contains the following features to help you deliver the unit.

The **Unit plan** summarises the topics covered in the unit, including the number of learning hours recommended for the topic, an outline of the learning content and the Cambridge resources that can be used to deliver the topic.

Topic	Approximate number of learning hours	Outline of learning content	Resources
1.4 Diseases	3–4	Organisms that cause diseases; body defences against disease; ways to control the spread of diseases	**Learner's Book:** Activity 1: Find information about diseases Activity 2: Group methods to prevent diseases Think like a scientist 1: Analyse hygiene methods that people use **Workbook:** Topic 1.4 ⬇ Worksheets 1.4 **Digital Classroom:** Video – Living things that cause disease

The **Background knowledge** feature explains prior knowledge required to access the unit and gives suggestions for addressing any gaps in your learners' prior knowledge.

Learners' prior knowledge can be informally assessed through the **Getting started** feature in the Learner's Book.

The **Teaching skills focus** feature covers a teaching skill and suggests how to implement it in the unit.

BACKGROUND KNOWLEDGE

The human body consists of a number of different systems that work together so that we can survive. At all times different body systems work together on specific jobs. These different body systems depend on one another.

TEACHING SKILLS FOCUS

Graphic organisers

Many learners find that using visual material, such as charts and diagrams, helps them to learn more effectively. Graphic organisers are visual illustrations of concepts and information.

Reflecting the Learner's Book, each unit consists of multiple sections. A section covers a learning topic.

At the start of each section, the **Learning plan** table includes the learning objectives, learning intentions and success criteria that are covered in the section.

It can be helpful to share learning intentions and success criteria with your learners at the start of a lesson so that they can begin to take responsibility for their own learning

LEARNING PLAN

Learning objectives	Learning intentions	Success criteria
6Bs.01 Describe the human circulatory system in terms of the heart pumping blood through arteries, capillaries and veins, describe its function (limited to transporting oxygen, nutrients and waste) and know that many vertebrates have a similar circulatory system.	• Describe the parts of the circulatory system and their functions.	• Learners can describe the parts of the circulatory system and their functions.

There are often **common misconceptions** associated with particular learning topics. These are listed, along with suggestions for identifying evidence of the misconceptions in your class and suggestions for how to overcome them.

Misconception	How to identify	How to overcome
Blood in the veins is blue, due to diagrams of the circulatory system showing the veins in blue.	Ask learners how the blood in the arteries and veins is different and why they think so.	Explain that the blood in both the arteries and veins is red but the blood in the veins is darker red as it carries very little oxygen. (The exception is the pulmonary veins from the lungs.)

For each topic, there is a selection of **starter ideas**, **main teaching ideas** and **plenary ideas**. You can pick out individual ideas and mix and match them depending on the needs of your class. The activities include suggestions for how they can be differentiated or used for assessment. **Homework ideas** are also provided.

Starter idea

1 **Getting started (15–20 minutes)**

Resources: Learner's Book. Each learner will need paper and coloured pencils

Description: The activity will help identify the misconception that the lungs are hollow and inflate and deflate like a balloon when we inhale and exhale.

Main teaching ideas

2 **How much air do we breathe in and out? (30–40 minutes)**

Learning intention: To find out how much air our lungs can hold.

Resources: One balloon per learner

Per group: a tape measure or length of string, a marking pen and a ruler

Description: Learners will exhale into a balloon and measure the size of the blown-up balloon. This will give them an idea of how much air their lungs can hold.

The **Language support** feature contains suggestions for how to support learners with English as an additional language. The vocabulary terms and definitions from the Learner's Book are also collected here.

LANGUAGE SUPPORT

Write the new words for the topic on the board. Say the words out aloud so learners know how the words sound.

Learners will use the following words:

breathing: the way we take air into our lungs and let it out again

The **Cross-curricular links** feature provides suggestions for linking to other subject areas.

CROSS-CURRICULAR LINKS

You can link making a model to explain breathing in Main teaching idea 2 with Arts and crafts and Design.

Recording data in tables and drawing graphs in Main teaching ideas 3 links with data handling and graphing in Maths.

> **Digital Classroom:** If you have access to Digital Classroom, these links will suggest when to use the various multimedia enhancements and interactive activities.

Digital resources to download

This Teacher's Resource includes a range of digital materials that you can download from Cambridge GO. (For more information about how to access and use your digital resource, please see inside front cover.) This icon ⬇ indicates material that is available from Cambridge GO.

Helpful documents for planning include:

- **Letter for parents – Introducing the Cambridge Primary resources:** a template letter for parents, introducing the Cambridge Primary Science resources.
- **Lesson plan template:** a Word document that you can use for planning your lessons. Examples of completed lesson plans are also provided.
- **Curriculum framework correlation:** a table showing how the Cambridge Primary Science resources map to the Cambridge Primary Science curriculum framework.
- **Scheme of work:** a suggested scheme of work that you can use to plan teaching throughout the year.

Each unit includes:

- **Differentiated worksheets:** these worksheets are provided in variations that cater for different abilities. Worksheets labelled 'A' are intended to support less confident learners, worksheets labelled 'B' should cater for the majority of learners, while worksheets labelled 'C' are designed to challenge more confident learners. For some worksheets, 'Help' and 'Stretch' sheets are provided in addition to the worksheet activity, which can be given to less confident or more confident learners as appropriate. Answer sheets are provided.
- **Language worksheets:** these worksheets provide language support and can be particularly helpful for learners with English as an additional language. Answers sheets are provided.
- **Resource sheets:** these include templates and any other materials that support activities described in the teaching notes.
- **End-of-unit tests:** these provide quick checks of the learner's understanding of the concepts covered in the unit. Answers are provided. Advice on using these tests formatively is given in the Assessment for Learning section of this Teacher's Resource.

Additionally, the Teacher's Resource includes:

- **Diagnostic check and answers:** a test to use at the beginning of the year to discover the level that learners are working at. The results of this test can inform your planning.
- **Mid-year test and answers:** a test to use after learners have studied half the units in the Learner's Book. You can use this test to check whether there are areas that you need to go over again.
- **End-of-year test and answers:** a test to use after learners have studied all units in the Learner's Book. You can use this test to check whether there are areas that you need to go over again, and to help inform your planning for the next year.
- **Answers to Learner's Book questions**
- **Answers to Workbook questions**
- **Glossary**

In addition, you can find more detailed information about teaching approaches.

Video is available through the Digital Classroom.

4 FOOD CHAINS AND FOOD WEBS

Plenary ideas

1 I can and I know (5–10 minutes)

Resources: Learners will need paper and pens or pencils

Description: This activity does not appear in the Learner's Book.

Ask learners to each write two sentences about what they have learnt in the topic. Their sentences should start with either:

I can …

or

I know …

Give learners one or two minutes to write their sentences. Then write or project a list of success criteria onto the board. Learners can compare their sentences with the success criteria to assess if they have grasped the main ideas and skills covered in the topic.

> **Assessment ideas:** This is a self-assessment activity which will help learners to identify areas where they are succeeding or where they

CROSS-CURRICULAR LINKS

Recording data in a table and drawing a graph in Main teaching idea 2 links with data handling and graphing in Maths.

Writing answers to questions throughout the topic can be linked with sentence construction and vocabulary development in English.

Homework ideas

Learners could complete the Focus, Practice and/or Challenge Exercises for the topic in the Workbook, depending on their progress.

In the next lesson, discuss answers. Learners can work in pairs to check one another's answers.

2 Learners could answer the questions at the end of Main teaching idea 2, Think like a scientist: Play a food chain game. Discuss answers in class and allow learners to check their own work and make any corrections needed.

PRIMARY SCIENCE 6 UNIT 1: THE HUMAN BODY

...et 1.2

...ory system

...e parts of the respiratory system on the outline below.

...to compare breathing in and breathing out.

Breathing in	
Breathing out	

...ss 2021

5

Name _____   Date ____

End-of-unit 1 test

The End-of-unit tests have been written by the authors. These may not fully refle...
Cambridge Assessment International Education.

...system i...

1 Name the three types of blood ve... from biggest to smallest in size.

   • _____
   • _____
   • _____

2 Which of these statements abo...
Tick the correct box for each st...

Statement		
a	The heart is made o...	
b	The heart has to s...	
c	The left side of the... oxygen.	
d	The right side of... oxygen.	
e	The ribs protect...	

Cambridge Primary Science...

BACKGROUND KNOWLEDGE

Food webs

Learners should already know that plants produce their own food using energy from the Sun and are, therefore, known as producers. Animals eat or consume plants and other animals to obtain the energy they need. Animals are, therefore, consumers. Food chains show the direction of energy transfer from one living thing to another. A food chain is a drawing representing feeding relationships and energy transfers between living things.

However, the transfer of energy in ecosystems is much more complex than in a single food chain. Most consumers eat more than one other species of plant or animal. Producers are usually eaten by many different herbivores or omnivores. Most herbivores are eaten by more than one carnivore or omnivore. A food web shows all the possible food chains a living thing can be part of in its habitat and is, therefore, a more accurate representation of energy transfers between organisms.

Each feeding level in a food chain is known as a trophic level. Energy transfers between trophic levels in food chains and food webs are not efficient. On average, only about 10% of the energy present in one trophic level is transferred to the next trophic level. The remaining 90% of the energy moves out of the food

chain to the surroundings as heat or is used by the organism itself for growth, movement, reproduction and other life processes. As a result of the decreasing quantity of energy available to each successive trophic level, there are usually no more than five trophic levels in food chains. There are also fewer individuals at the end of food chains, for the same reason.

Threats to food chains and food webs from toxic substances

Polluting chemicals sometimes enter food chains, either accidentally in the case of spills, or on purpose, such as with fertilisers and pesticides. Many of these... ...es are harmful or toxic. Some toxic chem... ...mless substances in the... ...l... he... so... th... ab... fo... th... d...

TEACHING SKILLS FOCUS

Reflective teaching

In each topic of the Learner's Book, learners have the opportunity to reflect on their learning and to think about what they are pleased with and how they could do things differently next time in order to improve their learning. The reflection process can also be valuable for teachers to consider what they do in the classroom, think about why they do it and if it works.

The process of reflective teaching is an ongoing one with four steps:

1 Teach

2 Consider the effect of your teaching on learning. For example:
   • What made the lesson go well? Why was it successful?

...sheet

...onsolidates the main ideas from Topics
...ners work in groups to construct a food
...ives and string, and simulate the effects
...stance on the food chain in their food
...d to make a set of food web cards to
... and different plants and animals.

...to two or three groups of 10 to 15 each.
...up has cards to represent the Sun,
...res and carnivores. There are card
...d with Worksheet 4.2 for you to use.

...d be able to complete questions 1–4.
...rt to learners who need support in
...der in which the different living things
... More confident learners can attempt
...s 5 and 6 on the Stretch sheet.

Common misconceptions

Misconception	How to identify	How to overcome
Using antibacterial soaps and cleaning products will kill all microbes that cause diseases	Ask learners if their families use antibacterial soaps and cleaning products, or if they have seen these products advertised on TV. Why do people use these products?	Once you have taught the section about organisms that cause diseases, point out that not all diseases are caused by bacteria. This means that antibacterial soaps and cleaning products will not prevent diseases caused by viruses or fungi, for example.

Starter ideas

1 Getting started (10–15 minutes)

Resources: Learner's Book

Description: Ask learners to look at the picture and read the questions in the Learner's Book.

Learners should use their own life experiences and prior knowledge from Stage 4 about infectious diseases to answer the questions.

Use the 'Think-pair-share' method to allow learners to think about their answers for a minute or two, then discuss their answers with a partner before sharing their answers with the class.

2 Brainstorm: how to prevent infectious diseases (10–15 minutes)

Description: Recap with the class what an infectious disease is – a disease that is caused by a living thing (germ) that enters the body and makes you ill.

Have a group brainstorm session for learners to give their ideas of how we can prevent infectious diseases. Write their answers on the board. Learners may mention vaccinations, which they learnt about in Stage 4. Other answers may include washing hands, cooking food properly, not coughing or sneezing over others. You could mention the importance of washing hands in preventing the spread of diseases such as Ebola and Covid-19, which learners will probably have heard of.

If learners do not mention using antibacterial soaps and cleaning products, you can ask them why people use these products. Answers will show whether any learners have the misconception referred to above.

Learners could finish by acting out the modelling exercise from Worksheet 1.4, which shows what

happens if there are no measures to prevent diseases spreading.

Main teaching ideas

1 Questions about living things that cause diseases (10–15 minutes; allow an additional 30–40 minutes if you invite an outside speaker to your lesson.)

Learning intention: To find out about living things that cause diseases.

Resources: Learner's Book

> **Digital classroom:** Video: Living things that cause disease (optional). Alternatively, search the internet for images you can use, using terms such as 'cholera bacteria', 'flu virus', 'ringworm fungus' and 'malaria parasite'.

Description: Discuss the different types of living things that cause diseases.

> **Digital classroom:** If you have access to the Digital Classroom component, show the video 'Living things that cause disease', which has slides of disease-causing bacteria, viruses, fungi and other parasites. The i button will explain how to use the video.

Alternatively, show images that you have found yourself, such as pictures of the coronavirus that caused the worldwide Covid-19 disease outbreak in 2019 and 2020.

Learners should read the information in the Learner's Book before answering the questions individually.

To address the Science in Context strand in the curriculum, you could ask a health care worker to speak to the class about some common infectious diseases and how to prevent them. Follow up with a

---

> About the curriculum framework

The information in this section is based on the Cambridge Primary Science curriculum framework (0097) from 2020. You should always refer to the appropriate curriculum framework document for the year of your learners' assessment to confirm the details and for more information.
*Visit **www.cambridgeinternational.org/primary** to find out more.*

The Cambridge Primary Science curriculum framework has been updated for teaching from September 2021. The Cambridge Primary Science curriculum framework has been developed to support learners in building their understanding about the natural world, particularly how to explain and investigate phenomena.

The curriculum framework incorporates three components:

- four content strands (Biology, Chemistry, Physics, and Earth and Space)
- a skills strand called Thinking and Working Scientifically
- a context strand called Science in Context

Biology, Chemistry, Physics and Earth and Space provide the scientific knowledge content, which gradually develops from Stage 1 to Stage 6 and provides a smooth progression towards Cambridge Lower Secondary study.

The Thinking and Working Scientifically learning objectives focus on the key scientific skills that are developed throughout the course. This strand is split into five types of scientific enquiry:

- observing over time
- identifying and classifying
- pattern seeking
- fair testing, and
- research

Science in Context allows for personal, local and global contexts to be incorporated into scientific study, making science relevant to the contexts that learners are familiar with. This element of the curriculum framework offers great flexibility to teachers and learners around the world.

The Cambridge Primary Science curriculum framework promotes a learner-led, enquiry-based approach. Practical work is a valuable part of science learning and develops learners' investigation skills, such as observation, measurement and equipment handling.

⟩About the assessment

Information about the assessment of the Cambridge Primary Science curriculum framework is available on the Cambridge Assessment International Education website. www.cambridgeinternational.org/primary

⟩Approaches to learning and teaching

The following are the key pedagogies underpinning our course content and how we understand and define them.

Active learning

Active learning is a pedagogical practice that places student learning at its centre. It focuses on how students learn, not just on what they learn. We, as teachers, need to encourage learners to 'think hard', rather than passively receive information. Active learning encourages learners to take responsibility for their learning and supports them in becoming independent and confident learners in school and beyond.

Assessment for Learning

Assessment for Learning (AfL) is a teaching approach that generates feedback which can be used to improve learners' performance. Learners become more involved in the learning process and, from this, gain confidence in what they are expected to learn and to what standard. We, as teachers, gain insights into a learner's level of understanding of a particular concept or topic, which helps to inform how we support their progression.

Differentiation

Differentiation is usually presented as a teaching practice where teachers think of learners as individuals and learning as a personalised process. Whilst precise definitions can vary, typically the core aim of differentiation is viewed as ensuring that all learners, no matter their ability, interest or context, make progress towards their learning outcomes.

It is about using different approaches and appreciating the differences in learners to help them make progress. Teachers, therefore, need to be responsive, and willing and able to adapt their teaching to meet the needs of their learners.

Language awareness

For many learners, English is an additional language. It might be their second or perhaps their third language. Depending on the school context, students might be learning all or just some of their subjects through English. For all learners, regardless of whether they are learning through their first language or an additional language, language is a vehicle for learning. It is through language that students access the learning intentions of the lesson and communicate their ideas. It is our responsibility, as teachers, to ensure that language doesn't present a barrier to learning.

Metacognition

Metacognition describes the processes involved when learners plan, monitor, evaluate and make changes to their own learning behaviours. These processes help learners to think about their own learning more explicitly and ensure that they are able to meet a learning goal that they have identified themselves or that we, as teachers, have set.

Skills for Life

How do we prepare learners to succeed in a fast-changing world? To collaborate with people from around the globe? To create innovation as technology increasingly takes over routine work? To use advanced thinking skills in the face of more complex challenges? To show resilience in the face of constant change? At Cambridge, we are responding to educators who have asked for a way to understand how all these different approaches to life skills and competencies relate to their teaching. We have grouped these skills into six main Areas of Competency that can be incorporated into teaching, and have examined the different stages of the learning journey and how these competencies vary across each stage.

These six key areas are:

- Creativity – finding new ways of doing things, and solutions to problems
- Collaboration – the ability to work well with others
- Communication – speaking and presenting confidently and participating effectively in meetings
- Critical thinking – evaluating what is heard or read, and linking ideas constructively
- Learning to learn – developing the skills to learn more effectively
- Social responsibilities – contributing to social groups, and being able to talk to and work with people from other cultures.

Cambridge learner and teacher attributes

This course helps develop the following Cambridge learner and teacher attributes.

Cambridge learners	Cambridge teachers
Confident in working with information and ideas – their own and those of others.	Confident in teaching their subject and engaging each student in learning.
Responsible for themselves, responsive to and respectful of others.	Responsible for themselves, responsive to and respectful of others.
Reflective as learners, developing their ability to learn.	Reflective as learners themselves, developing their practice.
Innovative and equipped for new and future challenges.	Innovative and equipped for new and future challenges.
Engaged intellectually and socially, ready to make a difference.	Engaged intellectually, professionally and socially, ready to make a difference.

Reproduced from Developing the Cambridge learner attributes *with permission from Cambridge Assessment International Education.*

More information about these approaches to learning and teaching is available to download from Cambridge GO (as part of this Teacher's Resource).

> Setting up for success

Our aim is to support better learning in the classroom with resources that allow for increased learner autonomy while supporting teachers to facilitate student learning.

Through an active learning approach of enquiry-led tasks, open-ended questions and opportunities to externalise thinking in a variety of ways, learners will develop analysis, evaluation and problem-solving skills.

Some ideas to consider to encourage an active learning environment are as follows:

- Set up seating to make group work easy.

- Create classroom routines to help learners to transition between different types of activity efficiently, e.g. move from pair work to listening to the teacher to independent work.

- Source mini-whiteboards, which allow you to get feedback from all learners rapidly.

- Start a portfolio for each learner, keeping key pieces of work to show progress at parent–teacher days.

- Have a display area with learners' work and vocab flashcards.

Planning for active learning

We recommend the following approach to planning. A blank Lesson Plan Template is available to download to help with this approach.

1 **Plan learning intentions and success criteria:** these are the most important feature of the lesson. Teachers and learners need to know where they are going in order to plan a route to get there.

2 **Plan language support:** think about strategies to help learners overcome the language demands of the lesson so that language doesn't present a barrier to learning.

3 **Plan starter activities:** include a 'hook' or starter to engage learners using imaginative strategies. This should be an activity where all learners are active from the start of the lesson.

4 **Plan main activities:** during the lesson, try to: give clear instructions, with modelling and written support; coordinate logical and orderly transitions between activities; make sure that learning is active and all learners are engaged ; create opportunities for discussion around key concepts.

5 **Plan assessment for learning and differentiation:** use a wide range of Assessment for Learning techniques and adapt activities to a wide range of abilities. Address misconceptions at appropriate points and give meaningful oral and written feedback which learners can act on.

6 **Plan reflection and plenary:** at the end of each activity and at the end of each lesson, try to: ask learners to reflect on what they have learnt since the beginning of the lesson; build on and extend this learning.

7 **Plan homework:** if setting homework, it can be used to consolidate learning from the previous lesson or to prepare for the next lesson.

To help planning using this approach, a blank Lesson plan template is available to download from Cambridge GO (as part of this Teacher's Resource). There are also examples of completed lesson plans.

For more guidance on setting up for success and planning, please explore the Professional Development pages of our website **www.cambridge.org/education/PD**

> 1 The human body

Unit plan

Topic	Approx. number of learning hours	Outline of learning content	Resources
1.1 The circulatory system	4–5	• The parts of the circulatory system and their functions	**Learner's Book:** Activity 1: Compare circulatory systems of some vertebrates Think like a scientist 1: Measuring pulse rate Think like a scientist 2: How does exercise affect pulse rate? Activity 2: Identify other factors that affect pulse rate Think like a scientist 3: Ask and investigate a question **Workbook:** Topic 1.1 ⬇ Worksheet 1.1 **Digital Classroom:** Activity – The human body Video – The circulatory system Video – How does exercise affect pulse rate? Manipulative – Heartbeat and exercise
1.2 The respiratory system	3–4	• The main parts of the respiratory system and their functions	**Learner's Book:** Activity 1: Investigate breathing Think like a scientist 1: Make a model to explain breathing Activity 2: Find out how other animals get oxygen Think like a scientist 2: Investigate breathing rate **Workbook:** Topic 1.2 ⬇ Worksheet 1.2 **Digital Classroom:** Video – The respiratory system
1.3 The reproductive system	2–3	• Body changes in puberty; the main parts of the reproductive system and their functions	**Learner's Book:** Activity: What do you know or want to know about puberty? **Workbook:** Topic 1.3
1.4 Diseases	3–4	• Organisms that cause diseases; body defences against disease; ways to control the spread of diseases	**Learner's Book:** Activity 1: Find information about diseases Activity 2: Group methods to prevent diseases Think like a scientist: Analyse hygiene methods that people use **Workbook:** Topic 1.4 ⬇ Worksheet 1.4 **Digital Classroom:** Video – Living things that cause disease

Across unit resources		
Learner's Book:	**Teacher's Resource:**	**Digital Classroom:**
Project: The circulatory system	⬇ Language worksheets 1 and 2	End-of-unit quiz
Check your progress quiz	⬇ Diagnostic test	
	⬇ Mid-year test	
	⬇ End-of-year test	
	⬇ End-of-unit test	

BACKGROUND KNOWLEDGE

Body systems

The human body consists of a number of different systems that work together so that we can survive. At all times different body systems work together on specific jobs. These different body systems depend on one another. This unit focuses on the circulatory system, respiratory system and reproductive system. The table summarises the main parts and functions of these systems. Diagrams of the body systems can be found in the Learner's Book.

System	Main parts	Functions
Circulatory	heart, blood and blood vessels (arteries, veins and capillaries)	transports food and oxygen to all body organs and tissues and removes wastes such as carbon dioxide
Respiratory	nose and mouth, trachea (windpipe) and other air passageways (bronchi), lungs and diaphragm muscle	carries air into and out of the lungs where gases (oxygen and carbon dioxide) are exchanged
Reproductive	ovaries, oviducts, uterus, birth canal (vagina) in females

testes, sperm ducts, penis in males | forms sex cells (ova in females; sperm in males) which join during fertilisation to form a new individual |

Puberty

Puberty is linked to the development of the reproductive system in boys and girls. Puberty happens to everyone, although it may occur at different ages, sometimes starting at the early age of 8 or 9 in girls or as late as 14 or 15 in boys. Puberty is caused by the action of hormones produced in the body.

Puberty is a time when a person's body, feelings and relationships change from those of a child to an adult's. These changes are physical, emotional and social. The physical changes that occur during puberty are discussed in the Learner's Book. It is also important to know that while the body is changing, so are the feelings and relationships a person has. Learners need to know that no matter when the changes of puberty happen to them, they are all normal.

Diseases

Infectious diseases are caused by micro-organisms that enter the body and grow and reproduce there. The micro-organisms that cause disease include bacteria, viruses, fungi and other parasitic organisms such as the malaria parasite. Disease-causing organisms are called pathogens.

The body has a number of defence mechanisms to prevent infection by pathogens. This unit looks at the frontline defences, namely the skin, stomach and body secretions such as mucus and tears. The spread of diseases can be controlled by good hygiene and the prevention of bites by insects that spread disease.

TEACHING SKILLS FOCUS

Graphic organisers

Many learners find that using visual material, such as charts and diagrams, helps them to learn more effectively. Graphic organisers are visual illustrations of concepts and information. Graphic organisers provide a picture of key ideas and information on a topic and the relationship of the parts to one another and to the whole. Graphic organisers are also useful when brainstorming ideas, especially as part of a group project or planning activity. Flow charts, Venn diagrams and mind maps are examples of graphic organisers.

Venn diagrams consist of two or three overlapping labelled circles. Each circle has its own subject, written as a heading or title, e.g. type of blood vessel. Within the overlap area, learners write the things that the different subjects have in common, such as carry blood. Features that are not shared are placed where the circles do not overlap. Venn diagrams are useful for tasks which require making comparisons of features or properties.

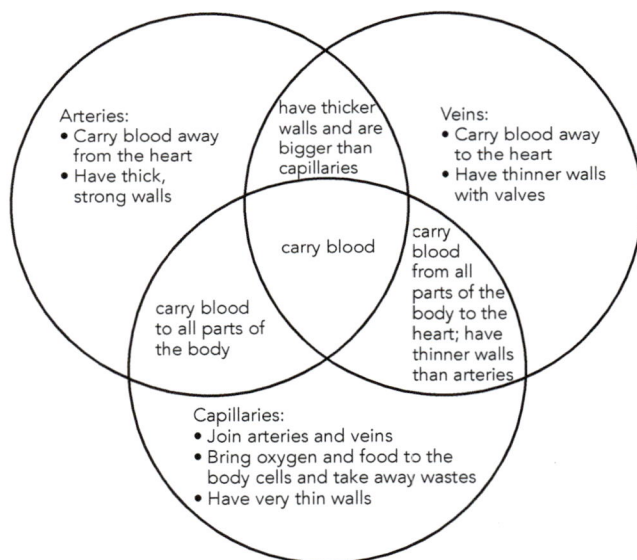

K-W-L (Know, Want to Know, Learnt) charts are divided into three columns titled 'Know', 'Want to know' and 'Learnt'. The chart helps to guide learners through a lesson or topic. It helps you to establish learners' prior knowledge about the topic and to find out which aspects of the topic learners are most interested in. For example, for a lesson on the heart, learners would write what they know about the heart in the 'Know' column, e.g. 'I know the heart beats

all the time. I know the heart is made of muscle'. In the 'Want to Know' column, learners write what they want to learn, e.g. 'Why does the heart beat? Does the heart ever rest?' Once the lesson is completed, learners write in the 'Learnt' column what they actually learnt about the heart

K-W-L chart		
What I know	What I want to know	What I learnt

Flow charts show the steps in a process using boxes connected with arrows. Flow charts can be used to plan the steps in an investigation or summarise the steps in process. Cycle diagrams can be used in the same way as flow charts to show processes that repeat themselves in a cycle.

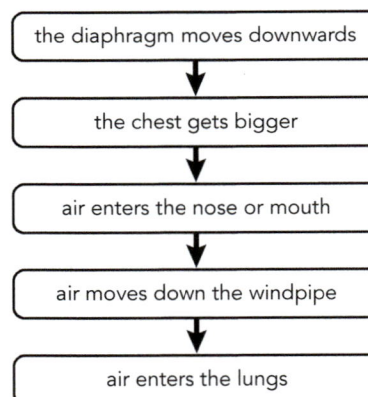

Look for other opportunities in this unit to use various graphic organisers with your class.

1.1 The circulatory system

Learning objectives	Learning intentions	Success criteria
6Bs.01 Describe the human circulatory system in terms of the heart pumping blood through arteries, capillaries and veins, describe its function (limited to transporting oxygen, nutrients and waste) and know that many vertebrates have a similar circulatory system.	• Describe the parts of the circulatory system and their functions.	• Learners can describe the parts of the circulatory system and their functions.
Bs.01 Describe the human circulatory system in terms of the heart pumping blood through arteries, capillaries and veins, describe its function (limited to transporting oxygen, nutrients and waste) and know that many vertebrates have a similar circulatory system.	• Learn that the circulatory systems of other animals are similar to ours.	• Learners can say how the circulatory systems of other animals are similar to ours.
6TWSp.02 Know the features of the five main types of scientific enquiry	• To identify the type/s of scientific enquiry used in an investigation.	• Learners can say how the circulatory systems of other animals are similar to ours.
6TWSc.08 Collect and record observations and/or measurements in tables and diagrams appropriate to the type of scientific enquiry.	• To record results in tables.	• Learners can record results in tables.
6TWSp.04 Plan fair test investigations, identifying the independent, dependent and control variables.	• To plan a fair test on the effect of exercise on pulse rate.	• Learners can plan a fair test on the effect of exercise on pulse rate.
6TWSp.03 Make predictions, referring to relevant scientific knowledge and understanding within familiar and unfamiliar contexts.	• To make a prediction about how exercise affects pulse rate.	• Learners can make a prediction about how exercise affects pulse rate.
6TWSa.01 Describe the accuracy of predictions, based on results.	• To use results to say if the prediction was accurate.	• Learners can use results to say if the prediction was accurate.
6TWSa.02 Describe patterns in results, including identifying any anomalous results.	• To describe any patterns in results.	• Learners can describe any patterns in results.
6TWSa.03 Make a conclusion from results informed by scientific understanding.	• To use results to make a conclusion.	• Learners can use results to make a conclusion.

CONTINUED

Learning objectives	Learning intentions	Success criteria
6TWSc.07 Use a range of secondary information sources to research and select relevant evidence to answer questions.	• To find information to answer a scientific question.	• Learners can find information to answer a scientific question.
6TWSp.01 Ask scientific questions and select appropriate scientific enquiries to use.	• To ask a question to investigate and find the answer.	• Learners can ask a question to investigate and find the answer.
6TWSm.02 Use models, including diagrams, to represent and describe scientific phenomena and ideas.	• To make a model to demonstrate how the heart works.	• Learners can make a model to demonstrate how the heart works.

LANGUAGE SUPPORT

Learners will use the following words:

blood: a red liquid that carries food and oxygen to all parts of the body

blood vessels: special tubes that carry the blood

carbon dioxide: a waste gas that the body must get rid of

circulation: the pumping of blood all around the body

circulatory system: the system formed by the heart, blood vessels and blood to carry food and oxygen around the body

heart: the special muscle that pumps blood around the body

oxygen: a gas in the air that the body uses

pulse: a small beat felt under the skin due to the pressure of blood as the heart pumps it around the body

pressure: the force that is exerted on or against an object by something in contact with it, for example, when we squeeze water out of a sponge, we exert pressure on the sponge

Where possible, use familiar examples or contexts to explain the words. For example, learners will know that a circle is round. Explain that when blood circulates, it moves round and round the body in a certain pathway.

Explain that a vessel is a container for something, usually a liquid, for example a jug. The blood vessels contain the liquid blood. Vessel is also used to describe a sailing ship.

Common misconceptions

Misconception	How to identify	How to overcome
Blood in the veins is blue, due to diagrams of the circulatory system showing the veins in blue.	Ask learners how the blood in the arteries and veins is different and why they think so.	Explain that the blood in both the arteries and veins is red but the blood in the veins is darker red as it carries very little oxygen. (The exception is the pulmonary veins from the lungs.)

Starter ideas

1 Getting started (10–15 minutes)

Resources: Learner's Book; Digital Classroom: Activity: The human body (optional) or a human body outline per pair

Description: This activity draws on learners' existing knowledge about body organs from Stages 3 and 4.

Tell learners to work in pairs to read and answer the questions in the Learner's Book.

Give each pair an outline of the human body. Ask them to draw in and label on the outline the organs they named in the questions.

You can ask them to put up their hands to volunteer to share their answers and show their filled-in body outlines.

Ask the class to give their opinions of the answers given. Do they agree with the answers? Would they like to share any of their own ideas about the answers?

> **Digital Classroom:** If you have access to the Digital Classroom component, use the activity 'The human body' to revise and establish learners' knowledge of organs in the body. The i button will explain how to use the activity.

2 What can you hear? (10–15 minutes)

Resources: Each pair of learners will need the inner cardboard tube of a roll of kitchen paper towel (or toilet paper roll or paper cup with the bottom cut out)

Plastic washing-up liquid bottle filled with water.

Description: Have learners work in same gender pairs and put the inner cardboard tube of kitchen paper towel on the chest of their partner and listen. Tell them that they may move the tube around until they hear something. Ask learners what they hear and where they think the sound is coming from. Explain that the sound is the heart beating.

You can bring in the Science in Context strand of the curriculum by telling learners that the first stethoscope that was ever used to listen to the heart beating was a wooden tube. It was used in the same way as learners' card tubes. If possible, show the class what a modern stethoscope looks like or refer to the picture in the project for this unit in the Learner's Book.

Talk about what the heart does and how it does it.

Main teaching ideas

1 How the heart works (10 minutes)

Learning intention: To demonstrate how the heart works.

Resources: Plastic washing-up liquid bottle filled with water, red food colouring, dropper, basin

Description: This activity demonstrates how the heart works like a pump to push the blood all the way round the body. It is not found in the Learner's Book.

Learners will make a simple model from a plastic washing-up liquid bottle filled with water which they squeeze to simulate the pumping action of the heart.

Explain that by squeezing the bottle you put pressure on the water which makes it squirt out of the bottle. The heart works in the same way.

Challenge learners to squeeze the bottle as many times as they can in one minute. Are they able to squeeze it more than 70 times? Explain that this is how hard the heart has to work all the time.

> **Practical guidance:** Learners should work in pairs or small groups. They should fill a plastic washing-up liquid bottle with water. They can add a drop of red food colouring into the water to give it the same colour as blood.

Learners should squeeze the bottle to simulate the pumping action of the heart. They should do this over the basin to avoid spilling water on the desk. They should not point the bottle at another learner when they squeeze it. Learners will observe that the water is pushed out of the bottle with force.

> **Differentiation ideas:** More confident learners can do some research to find out why we can hear our heart beating. They should find out that the sound of the heartbeat is made by the pressure of the blood being squeezed out the heart when the muscle contracts.

2 Activity 1: Compare the circulatory systems of some vertebrates (20 minutes)

Learning intention: To learn that the circulatory systems of other animals are similar to ours.

Resources: Learner's Book; Worksheet 1.1 (optional)

> **Digital Classroom:** Video: The circulatory system (optional) or internet video clip on the circulatory system

Description: If you have access to the Digital Classroom component, show the video 'The circulatory system', which shows clips of the heart beating and blood flowing in the human circulatory system.

Alternatively, do an internet search for a video clip on the human heart and circulatory system. You can use search terms such as 'how your heart works' or 'the heart and circulatory system'. Show the video clip and discuss the way the circulatory system works.

Then let learners work in pairs to look carefully at the drawings of the circulatory systems of the fish, frog and bird in the Learner's Book.

Remind them to look for both similarities and differences in the circulatory systems compared to the human circulatory system.

Learners could then complete Worksheet 1.1 to consolidate their knowledge of the differences in heartbeats for different animals.

> **Differentiation ideas:** More confident learners could draw a Venn diagram to compare the different circulatory systems.

> **Assessment ideas:** Learners can answer the self-assessment questions at the end of the activity in the Learner's Book.

3 Think like a scientist 1: Measuring pulse rate (20–30 minutes)

Learning intentions: To measure pulse rate.

To identify the type of scientific enquiry used in an investigation.

Resources: Per group: a timer or a watch with a second hand or stopwatch

Description: Explain what pulse rate is. To link with the Science in Context strand of the curriculum, explain that doctors and other healthcare workers use pulse rate as a sign of illness. For example, a very fast pulse can be a sign of heart disease.

Tell learners to read through the instructions for the activity in the Learner's Book.

Ask learners to predict what they think their pulse rate will be. Don't expect answers to be accurate. Learners can compare their prediction with the actual measurements later on.

Learners' tables should record pulse rates of group members as well. They will be using the observing over time type of scientific enquiry.

> **Practical guidance:** Demonstrate to the class how to find their pulse.

Measure and record your own pulse rate on the board. Then measure a volunteer learner's pulse rate and record it too. Point out that the pulse rates are not the same. Various factors affect pulse rate. Age is one of them. Children have faster pulse rates at rest than adults. There is also normal variation between individuals of the same age, as learners will observe when they measure their own pulse rates.

> **Differentiation ideas:** You may need to assist some learners in calculating the group's average pulse rate. Explain that they should add up all the pulse rates they measured and then divide the total by the number of members in the group. Do an example on the board to aid your explanation.

4 Think like a scientist 2: How does exercise affect pulse rate? (45–60 minutes)

Learning intentions: To plan a fair test on the effect of exercise on pulse rate.

To make a prediction about how exercise affects pulse rate. To record results in a table. To use results to say if the prediction was accurate. To describe any patterns in results. To use results to make a conclusion. To identify the type/s of scientific enquiry used in an investigation.

Resources: Learner's Book

Per group: a timer or a watch with a second hand or stopwatch

> **Digital classroom:** Video: How does exercise affect pulse rate? (optional); Digital Classroom manipulative: Heartbeat and exercise (optional)

Description:

> **Digital classroom:** If you have access to the Digital Classroom component, show the video 'How does exercise affect pulse rate?' to help learners make their predictions. The i button will explain how to use the video. Ask learners if all the children in the screens will have the same pulse rates. Why or why not? Ask which person they think will have the highest pulse rate (child skipping) which person will have the lowest pulse rate (child sleeping) and why. Ask learners to rank the activities in the slides from the one resulting in highest pulse rate to the one resulting in lowest pulse rate (skipping, walking, writing, sleeping).

Alternatively, you can look for similar pictures in magazines or on the internet of people (preferably children) being active to use as a stimulus for the discussion.

Tell learners to read the instructions in the Learner's Book. Recap on the role of dependent, independent and control variables in a fair test investigation if you feel learners will need help with this. Refer to the 'Working like a scientist' section at the start of the Learner's Book. Learners will also be observing and measuring changes over time.

Remind learners that a conclusion is what we find out from the results of an investigation. Guide them by asking questions such as:

- What did you observe or measure?
- Why did this happen?
- What did you find out from your observations or results?

> **Digital Classroom:** If you have access to the Digital Classroom component, use the manipulative 'Heartbeat and exercise' to consolidate learners understanding at the end of the investigation. The i button will explain how to use the manipulative. As a follow up, you could ask learners to think about ways in which they could improve their investigation. They should explain why their suggestions would improve the investigation. For example, they could measure the pulse rates of more people to make their results more reliable. Some suggestions will depend on the design of the investigation.

> **Practical guidance:** This is a learner-led practical. Divide learners into groups of 4–5.

Allow about 15 minutes planning time. Ask the groups to show their plans to you. Guide them if their plans do not seem suitable.

> **Differentiation ideas:** Group learners in mixed-ability groups so that less confident learners can be encouraged and helped by more confident learners.

> **Assessment ideas:** You could use the following checklist to assess learners' investigations.

Assessment criteria	Well	Quite well	Needed help
How well did the learners…			
Make a prediction with reasons?			
Identify dependent, independent and control variables?			
Choose and use tables or diagrams to record results?			
Use the results to make a conclusion?			

Plenary ideas

1 What have you learnt? (5–10 minutes)

Description: Let learners stand and quickly say one thing that have learnt in the topic before sitting down.

> **Assessment ideas:** Learners' answers should give you a quick overview of how well the class has understood the work covered in the topic.

2 Exit tickets (5–10 minutes)

Resources: Exit tickets (see below)

Description: Make a set of 'exit' tickets to give to learners. Each card should have a question or sentence to complete on it. Learners have to hand you back a 'ticket' with an answer. Some examples are:

- Today I learnt…
- I would have liked…
- Now I understand… .

Reflection ideas: Learners can answer the Reflection questions at the end of the topic in the Learner's Book.

CROSS-CURRICULAR LINKS

Recording data in tables and drawing graphs in Main teaching ideas 2 and 3 links with data handling and graphing in Maths.

Investigating the effect of exercise on pulse rate in Main teaching idea 3 can be linked with Physical Education.

Reading and following written instructions and writing answer sentences can be linked with comprehension skills and sentence construction in English.

Homework ideas

1 Learners can make a mind map about what they have learnt about the circulatory system. In the next lesson, learners can explain their mind map to a partner. The partner can rate the mind map and explanation with one, two or three stars and say what they liked and what they think could be done better.

2 Learners could complete the Focus, Practice and / or Challenge Workbook exercises for the topic, depending on their progress.

In the next lesson, discuss answers in class. Allow learners to check their own work.

Topic Worksheet

Worksheet 1.1: Compare heartbeats

This worksheet is intended to help learners practise their skills in finding patterns in results and, for more confident learners, in making predictions based on the pattern identified.

All learners should be able to answer questions 1–4. Give the Help sheet to learners who need support in identifying patterns in results. More confident learners can attempt the additional questions on the Stretch sheet. They will need to do research to find and confirm answers.

1.2 The respiratory system

LEARNING PLAN

Learning objectives	Learning intentions	Success criteria
6Bs.02 Describe the human respiratory system in terms of oxygen from the air moving into the blood in the lungs, and know that many vertebrates have a similar respiratory system.	• To describe how the respiratory system works. • To show that breathing involves two different stages, breathing in and breathing out.	• Learners can describe how the respiratory system works. • Learners can show that breathing involves two different stages, breathing in and breathing out.
6TWSm.02 Use models, including diagrams, to represent and describe scientific phenomena and ideas.	• To make a model to explain breathing.	• Learners can make a model to explain breathing.
6TWSc.06 Carry out practical work safely.	• To do practical work safely.	• Learners can do practical work safely.
6TWSc.05 Take appropriately accurate measurements.	• To meas ure breathing rate.	• Learners can measure breathing rate.
6TWSc.08 Collect and record observations and/or measurements in tables and diagrams appropriate to the type of scientific enquiry.	• To record results in tables.	• Learners can record results in tables.
6TWSa.05 Present and interpret results using tables, bar charts, dot plots, line graphs and scatter graphs.	• To draw a line graph of results.	• Learners can draw a line graph of results.
6TWSa.03 Make a conclusion from results informed by scientific understanding.	• Use results to make a conclusion.	• Learners can use results to make a conclusion
6TWSc.07 Use a range of secondary information sources to research and select relevant evidence to answer questions.	• To find information to answer a scientific question.	• Learners can find information to answer a scientific question.

LANGUAGE SUPPORT

Learners will use the following words:

breathing: the way we take air into our lungs and let it out again

breathing rate: the number of times we breathe in and out in one minute

diaphragm: a muscle in the chest that helps us to breathe in and out

lungs: the organs we use for breathing

windpipe: the air tube that carries air from the nose and mouth to the lungs and back again

Help learners become more familiar with the terms by giving them starter sentences that use the terms, for example:

- The organs we use for breathing are the _____. (lungs)

- Our bodies need a gas in the air called _____. (oxygen)

- Our bodies produce a waste gas that we must get rid of called _____. (carbon dioxide)

- The air tube that carries the air we breathe in down to the lungs is the_____. (windpipe)

- The muscle in the chest that helps us to breathe in and out is the _____. (diaphragm) The number of times we breathe in and out in one minute is called the _____. (breathing rate)

Diaphragm is a word that learners may find difficult to pronounce. Sound it out for them – dai-uh-fram – and let them repeat it after you.

You should also point to the various parts of the respiratory system on a chart, model or slide when you introduce their names.

Common misconceptions

Misconception	How to identify	How to overcome
Teachers often use a balloon to demonstrate how the lungs expand and contract during breathing. This practice may lead learners to think that the lungs are hollow organs like balloons that can fill up with air when we inhale and collapse and empty when we exhale.	Ask learners to draw a picture of the lungs and to explain what happens to the lungs when we breathe in and out. (see Starter activity idea 1)	Use a bath sponge to explain to learners that the lungs are not hollow but are spongy and made up of numerous tiny air sacs, like the bath sponge. If possible, show a slide or video clip of the lungs.

Starter ideas

1 Getting started (15–20 minutes)

Resources: Learner's Book. Each learner will need paper and coloured pencils

Description: The activity will help identify the misconception that the lungs are hollow and inflate and deflate like a balloon when we inhale and exhale.

Learners should work on their own to draw their pictures.

Use the 'Think-pair-share' method to allow learners to draw their pictures and think about their answers for a minute or two. They then discuss their answers with a partner before sharing their answers with the class.

2 What do you already know about the respiratory system? (15–20 minutes)

Resources: Set of questions about the respiratory system

Description: This activity draws on learners' existing knowledge about the lungs and breathing.

Tell learners to work in pairs to read and answer the questions. Give learners a copy of the questions or project or write them on the board:

1 Which body organs do we use for breathing?
2 Where in the body are these organs found?
3 How many times do we breathe each minute?
4 Why do we need to breathe?
5 Do we breathe all the time? Say why or why not.

You can ask learners to put up their hands to volunteer to share their answers. Ask the class to give their opinions of the answers given. Do they agree with the answers? Would they like to share any of their own ideas about the answers?

Answers

1   The lungs.
2   In the chest.
3   Learners' own answers – usually around 15–20 times.
4   To take in air that contains oxygen which the body needs.
5   Yes. We need oxygen all the time, even when we are asleep.

Main teaching ideas

1   Activity 1: Investigate breathing (15–20 minutes)

Learning intention: To show that breathing involves two different stages, breathing in and breathing out.

Resources: Learner's Book

A balloon per learner

Measuring tape (optional)

Digital Classroom video : The respiratory system (optional) or search for video clips on the internet using 'how lungs work' or 'lungs and respiratory system'.

Description: Read through the instructions for the activity in the Learner's Book with the class. Demonstrate how to feel the difference between breathing in and breathing out. Show learners that they should place their hands with fingers forward and with thumbs pushed against the back of the ribs. They should breathe normally, then breathe more deeply and feel the difference. The ribs push out more with deeper breaths as the lungs expand more and fill with air.

> **Digital classroom:** If you have access to the Digital Classroom component, show the video 'The respiratory system'. The i button will explain how to use the video. Point out the different parts of the respiratory system and tell learners to observe how the lungs fill with air and expand when the diaphragm moves downwards as we breathe in. The opposite happens when we breathe out.

Alternatively, do an internet search for a video clip on the respiratory system. You can use search terms such 'how your lungs work' or 'the lungs and respiratory system'. Show the video clip and discuss the way the respiratory system works.

Learners should observe that the balloon inflates when they breathe out. This shows that air leaves our bodies when we breathe out.

> **Practical guidance:** Learners should work individually. The activity can be done at learners' desks. They should stand up, put their hands on their ribcage and breathe in and breathe out. You can demonstrate what to do in front of the class.

Learners should loosen up the balloon by blowing into it a few times. It is not recommended for health and hygiene reasons that learners share balloons. If you are not able to obtain a balloon for each learner, you can do a demonstration of breathing into a balloon for the class.

> **Differentiation ideas:** As an extension exercise for faster and more confident learners, you can get them to measure the difference in their chest diameter when they breathe in and out.

> **Assessment ideas:** Learners can pair up and explain to one another what happened when they breathed in and out. Then discuss answers in class.

2   How much air do we breathe in and out? (30–40 minutes)

Learning intention: To find out how much air our lungs can hold.

Resources: One balloon per learner

Per group: a tape measure or length of string, a marking pen and a ruler

Description: Learners will exhale into a balloon and measure the size of the blown-up balloon. This will give them an idea of how much air their lungs can hold.

Get groups to compare their measurements. Ask:

Did you notice any differences in the measurements?

What explanation can you suggest for these differences?

Why should we repeat measurements in an investigation?

Whose lungs can hold more air – a small child or a grown up?

Can you think of any other factors that could affect how much air we breathe in and out?

> **Practical guidance:** Divide learners into groups of boys only and girls only.

Learners should loosen up the balloon by blowing into it a few times.

They should inhale normally and then exhale normally into the balloon. Tell learners not to force their breathing.

They should pinch the open end of the balloon and get another group member to measure around the middle part of the balloon with the measuring tape or with the length of string. If using the string method, they should mark off the measurement with the length of string and then measure it on the ruler. Tell them to repeat this so that they have three measurements.

They should record the measurements in a data table and work out the average of the measurements.

Answers

Answers will depend on measurements made by learners.
They should observe that the measurements were higher for boys than for girls. They may also find that taller or bigger learners exhaled more air than shorter or smaller learners.
We repeat measurements to check that they are accurate and that we haven't made a mistake in the measuring.
A grown-up has bigger lungs than a small child and therefore holds more air in their lungs.
Other factors that could affect how much air we breathe in and out are physical fitness and illness.

> **Differentiation ideas:** Ask more confident learners to identify the different variables in the investigation: independent variable (sex of learner); dependent variable (size of balloon filled with exhaled air); control variables (type of balloon, method of measuring)

3   **Think like a scientist 1: Make a model to explain breathing (1 hour)**

Learning intentions: To describe how the respiratory system works.
To make and explain a model of breathing.
To do practical work safely.

Resources: Learner's Book
Per group: a plastic bottle; a narrow plastic tube or straw; an elastic band; scissors; two balloons; play dough, electrical tape, sticky putty or Plasticine®

Description: Remind learners that we make models to represent objects or processes that happen in real life.

Read through the instructions for the activity in the Learner's Book.

If learners are to provide their own materials, allow them a few days to collect the materials for the activity.

Make a model of your own to help you identify any difficulties learners may have when they make their own models, for example sealing the neck of the bottle so no air escapes. You can demonstrate your model to the class so they can see how their own models should work.

> **Practical guidance:** This a learner-led activity.

Learners should work in groups of 4–5.

Remind learners to work safely with scissors when cutting materials to make their models.

> **Assessment ideas:** Learners can use the checklist to assess other groups' models. You will need to give each group a copy of the checklist.

	Yes	Partly	No
Does the model show the parts of the respiratory system?			
Does the model work to show breathing in and breathing out?			
Does the model look neat and attractive?			
Can the group explain how the model shows the breathing process?			

4   **Think like a scientist 2: Investigate breathing rate (40 minutes)**

Learning intentions: To measure breathing rate.
To record results in a table.
To draw a line graph of results.
To use results to make a conclusion.

Resources: A timer or watch with a second hand per pair of learners
Learner's Book

Description: Tell learners to read the instructions for the activity in the Learner's Book.

In the investigation, learners will measure the change in breathing rate over time.

Be aware that, unlike heart rate, which can't be consciously controlled, you can consciously control your breathing rate. This may influence results. Often, the more someone is told to 'breathe naturally', the less natural their breathing becomes.

Learners should use the results to make a conclusion that exercise makes the breathing rate increase.

Remind learners that we use line graphs to record changes in a variable over time. If you need to revise drawing of line graphs, refer to the Skills reference section at the end of the Stage 5 Learner's Book.

> **Practical guidance:** This is a learner-led practical task.

Learners should work in pairs.

Learners can count the number of breaths taken per minute by observing the rise and fall of their partner's chests. Another way to do this is by the partner placing their own hand on their ribs to show the breathing movements.

It may be interesting to compare the pairs' results at the end of the lesson and see the range in breathing rates. You could talk about how factors such as age, gender and fitness affect the breathing rate.

To link with the Science in Context strand of the curriculum, you could discuss the harmful effects of air pollution on the respiratory system, for example increased cases of asthma, coughing, bronchitis and even lung cancer. You could also talk about ways to reduce air pollution, such as at a personal level walking or cycling instead of travelling in a car or bus. At a government level you could discuss the use of non-polluting sources of energy, such as solar and wind energy instead burning coal, oil or gas in power stations.

> **Differentiation ideas:** If any learners are still struggling with drawing line graphs, get them to work with a more confident peer who can assist them in drawing their graphs.

Learners of higher ability can answer this question: Why are the lungs the only body organs that can float? The answer is because they are made of very many air sacs.

> **Assessment ideas:** Discuss the answers in class and allow learners to check their own work and make any corrections needed.

Tell them to look at their incorrect answers and to think about why they gave those answers. This will help to identify any aspects of the work they may need more help with.

Plenary ideas

1 I can and I know (5–10 minutes)

Resources: Learners will need paper and pens or pencils

Description: Ask learners to each write two sentences about what they have learnt in the topic.

Their sentences should start with either:

I can…

or

I know…

Give learners one or two minutes to write their sentences. Then write or project a list of success criteria onto the board. Learners can compare their sentences with the success criteria to assess if they have grasped the main ideas and skills covered in the topic.

> **Assessment ideas:** This is a self-assessment activity which will help learners to identify areas where they are succeeding or where they need more support.

> **Reflection ideas:** Learners should ask themselves:

What things did I find easy to learn?

What did I find difficult?

How did I deal with the difficult things?

What would I like to know more about?

2 True or false? (10–15 minutes)

Resources: True or false statements about the respiratory system, for example:

- The organs used for breathing are the lungs (true).
- The ribs protect the lungs (true).
- When we breathe in, our chests get smaller to pull in the air (false, the chest expands).
- When we breathe in, the lungs fill with air (true).
- The lungs are hollow sacs, like balloons (false, they are spongy with lots of air spaces).
- Exercise make us breathe faster (true).
- We get rid of carbon dioxide when we breathe out (true).
- The diaphragm muscle contracts to make us breathe faster (false, the diaphragm muscle contracts to make the chest expand so there is more space for lungs to fill up with air).

Description: Write or project a list of statements about the respiratory system onto the board. Learners can work in pairs to decide if each of the statements about the respiratory system is true or false.

> **Assessment ideas:** Discuss answers and let learners check their own work.

> **Reflection ideas:** Learners can answer the Reflection question in the Learner's Book.

You can link making a model to explain breathing in Main teaching idea 2 with Arts and crafts and Design.

Recording data in tables and drawing graphs in Main teaching idea 3 links with data handling and graphing in Maths.

Investigating the effect of exercise on breathing rate in Main teaching idea 3 can be linked with Physical Education.

Writing answers to questions throughout the topic can be linked with sentence construction and vocabulary development in English.

Homework ideas

1 Learners could repeat the activity suggested in Main teaching idea 2 at home with family members. They should compare the measurements they make and look for any patterns in the results. Hold a short report-back session in the next lesson to discuss learners' findings.

2 Learners could complete some or all of Worksheet 1. Less confident learners could answer questions 1–4, with the aid of the Help sheet. More confident learners should attempt stretch questions 5 and 6.

Topic Worksheet

Worksheet 1.2: The respiratory system

This worksheet revises the parts and functions of the respiratory system.

All learners should be able to draw and label the parts of the respiratory system in question 1, compare breathing in and breathing out and explain why we need to breathe in question 2. The Help sheet will assist learners who need support for question 1.

More confident learners can attempt questions 3 and 4 on the Stretch sheet to further their knowledge about the respiratory system and demonstrate their understanding of the relationship between the circulatory system and the respiratory system.

1.3 The reproductive system

LEARNING PLAN		
Learning objectives	**Learning intentions**	**Success criteria**
6Bp.01 Describe the physical changes that take place during puberty in humans.	• To describe body changes that happen during puberty.	• Learners can describe body changes that happen during puberty.
6Bs.03 Name the parts of the human reproductive system.	• To name the parts of the reproductive system.	• Learners can name the parts of the reproductive system.

LANGUAGE SUPPORT
• Write the new words for the topic on the board. Say the words out aloud so learners know how the words sound. • Get learners to repeat the new words straight away after you introduce them.
• Encourage group or pair work in which learners have the opportunity to practise using new or difficult words for themselves after you have introduced the terms.

CONTINUED

The key terms for this topic are:

puberty: the age at which a person becomes able to reproduce

hormones: chemicals in the body that cause the body changes that happen during puberty

sperm: male sex cells

ova: female sex cells

reproductive system: the parts of the body that make the sex cells

fertilisation: the joining of a male sex cell and a female sex cell

menstruation: the release of an unfertilised egg with the lining of the uterus

Starter ideas

1 Getting started (10–15 minutes)

Resources: Learner's Book

Description: Ask learners to read the questions in the Learner's Book.

Learners should use their prior knowledge from Stages 3 and 5 about reproduction to answer the questions.

Use the 'Think-pair-share' method to allow learners to think about their answers for a minute or two, then discuss their answer with a partner before sharing their answers with the class.

2 How have you changed? (15–20 minutes)

Resources: Pictures of different stages of human development – baby, toddler, young child, older child, adolescent, adult, older adult, for example:

(Search the internet for images for 'stages of human development.)

Description: This activity will help learners to think about how our bodies develop and change as we get older.

Let learners work in same-sex pairs. Show them the pictures of the different stages of human development. Ask learners to talk about the changes they see in the pictures. Ask them how they have changed since they were born.

They will observe that they have grown, their body proportions have changed (babies have very big heads compared to the rest of their bodies), they

can do many more things now that they couldn't do as babies or young children, such as walk, run, feed and dress themselves, talk, read and write.

Ask learners to put up their hands to volunteer to share their answers. Choose four or five volunteers to share their answers. Write their answers on the board and discuss them with the class.

Main teaching ideas

1 Activity: What do you know or want to know about puberty? (15–20 minutes)

Learning intention: To describe body changes that happen during puberty.

Resources: Learner's Book

Cardboard box with lid

Description: This is a sensitive topic to deal with as many learners feel shy about the body changes they experience during puberty. Perhaps have an introductory discussion which focuses on positive aspects of growing up such as being more independent. You could also briefly discuss non-physical changes, such as changes in feelings and attitudes.

You may prefer to separate boys and girls to discuss the topic, depending on the teaching arrangement in your school.

Let learners read the questions in the Learner's Book. They can work individually to answer the questions.

Learners' questions for you are confidential and should be anonymous. They can ask more than one question if they wish. Remind them not to write their names on the piece of paper. You can put a box with a lid at the front of the class for learners to drop their questions into. Ask them to fold the paper before they put it in the question box. Tell learners that you will be reading their questions and preparing answers for the next lesson.

> **Assessment ideas:** Learners can answer the self-assessment questions in the 'How am I doing?' feature in the Learner's Book.

2 Find out more about puberty (15–20 minutes class time plus 30–40 minutes at home)

Learning intention: To find out about changes that happen in puberty.

Resources: Set of questions developed by learners

Description: Puberty can be a difficult and confusing time for young people. Not only are their bodies changing, but so are their thoughts and emotions. It can be reassuring to know that they are not the only ones to have gone through these changes. Although each generation has its own special set of concerns, some feelings and experiences are the same for every generation.

Learners should work individually or in pairs to think of a set of three or four questions to ask a parent or other older family member about their experiences of puberty. The questions should be ones the learners are most interested in and also be likely to encourage the adult to give honest answers. You should check learners' questions to make sure they are appropriate.

They should give the list of questions to the family member and allow them some time to think about their answers.

> **Differentiation ideas:** More confident learners can work in pairs or small groups to share their findings. They can make a puberty information sheet to guide other boys or girls as to what they can expect during this stage of their lives.

3 Draw a timeline of body changes and developments (15–20 minutes plus preparation time at home)

Learning intentions: To draw a timeline of body changes and development.

Resources: Learners' own pictures of themselves from babyhood until now

Description: To prepare, learners will need pictures of themselves from babyhood until now. They should ask a parent or caregiver to tell them how old they were in each picture. Discuss with the class the different features that have changed over the years.

Learners should note how they have changed in each of the pictures.

They should then draw a timeline of their development, e.g. starting to walk or talk, body changes, etc., and mark these events (including puberty if it has already started) on their timeline. Make sure that all the learners know how to draw a timeline.

Suggest to the learners that they make a table to represent their own data with column headings of 'year' and 'changed feature' as this will make it easier to draw the timeline.

Answers

Learners will observe that they have grown, their body proportions have changed (babies have very big heads compared to the rest of their bodies), they can do many more things now that they couldn't do as babies or young children, such as walk, run, feed and dress themselves, talk, read and write.

An example of a timeline is given. Bear in mind that learners' timelines will be individual and unique.

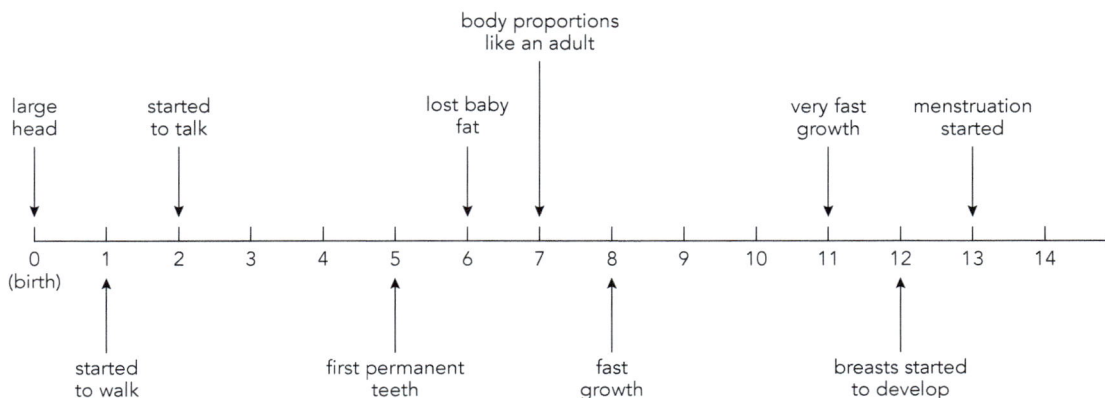

> **Differentiation ideas:** Some learners may need support in drawing a timeline. Remind them of the following:

- Draw a line across the page and divide it equally into the units of time you will use: the number of years of your life in this case.

- List the dates or times from left to right with the past on the left and the present on the right.

- On the timeline, mark the points where an important event happened. At each point draw a short line above or below the timeline and write a label to describe what happened at that time.

Draw an example on the board as a visual guide for learners.

> **Assessment ideas:** Use the checklist below to assess learners' timelines. Give learners feedback on their work and suggestions for any improvements.

Criteria	Yes	Partly	No
The learner:			
described how they had changed at different stages of their lives			
recorded their findings accurately in a table			
was able to process their data and draw an accurate timeline			

Plenary ideas

1 Activity: What did I learn? (10–20 minutes)

Resources: Pens and slips of paper or post-its

Description: Let learners each write down one thing that they have learnt in the topic. Collect learners' answers and select about ten to write on the board. Ask the class if each of the answers is correct and to say why or why not.

> **Assessment ideas:** Learners' answers should give you a quick overview of how well the class has understood the work covered in the topic.

2 Puberty review (10–15 minutes)

Resources: A set of statements about puberty on cards or written or projected onto the board

Examples of statements:

- Hair grows on face
- Hair gets oily
- Voice changes
- Breasts develop
- Grow taller
- Hair grows in armpits
- Hips get wider
- Shoulders get broader
- Menstruation begins

Description: Learners are shown a set of statements about puberty. They must say if each statement applies to girls, boys or both.

> **Assessment ideas:** Get learners to look in the Learner's Book and check if their answers are correct.

> **Reflection ideas:** Learners can answer the Reflection questions in the Learner's Book.

CROSS-CURRICULAR LINKS

Writing answers to questions throughout the topic can be linked with sentence construction and vocabulary development in English.

Homework ideas

1 Learners could complete the Focus, Practice and / or Challenge Workbook Exercises for the topic, depending on their progress.

   In the next lesson, discuss answers in class. Allow learners to check their own work.

2 Learners can make a summary table of the parts of the male and female reproductive systems and their functions.

   In the next lesson, discuss answers in class. Allow learners to swap answers and check each other's work.

1.4 Diseases

LEARNING PLAN

Learning objectives	Learning intentions	Success criteria
6Bp.02 Know that some diseases can be caused by infection with viruses, bacteria, parasites or fungi that can be passed from one host to another.	• Find out about types of living things that cause diseases.	• Learners can name living things that cause diseases.
6Bp.04 Know that humans have defence mechanisms against infectious diseases, including skin, stomach acid and mucus.	• Find out how our body stops us from getting infectious diseases.	• Learners can say how our body stops us from getting infectious diseases.
6Bp.03 Describe how good hygiene can control the spread of diseases transmitted in water, food and body fluids, and describe ways to avoid being bitten by insect vectors.	• Find out about things we can do to prevent diseases from spreading. • Learn how to avoid being bitten by insects.	• Learners can describe things we can do to prevent diseases from spreading. • Learners can say how to avoid being bitten by insects.
6TWSa.05 Present and interpret results using tables, bar charts, dot plots, line graphs and scatter graphs.	• To draw a dot plot of results.	• Learners can draw a dot plot of results.
6TWSc.01 Sort, group and classify objects, materials and living things through testing, observation and using secondary information.	• To group methods to prevent diseases.	• Learners can group methods to prevent diseases.

LANGUAGE SUPPORT

The new words for the topic are:

parasite: any living thing that lives on or in the body of another living thing

host: the living thing that a parasite infects. A host can also be a person who has guests, e.g. in their home or on a TV show

defence: protection against something, for example, using sunscreen is a defence against sunburn; the city walls were an important part of the city's defences long ago.

barrier: an object that stops things getting through or past it, for example a fence or a gate

mucus: sticky substance found in our noses, windpipe and other air passages

hygiene: keeping yourself and the things around you clean

vectors: living things that spread diseases but do not get the diseases themselves

repellent: a substance that keeps insects away

Some of the new words for the topic are used in everyday speech or writing. Give learners the opportunity to use these words correctly by asking them to write or complete sentences using the words.

Common misconceptions

Misconception	How to identify	How to overcome
Using antibacterial soaps and cleaning products will kill all microbes that cause diseases	Ask learners if their families use antibacterial soaps and cleaning products, or if they have seen these products advertised on TV. Why do people use these products?	Once you have taught the section about organisms that cause diseases, point out that not all diseases are caused by bacteria. This means that antibacterial soaps and cleaning products will not prevent diseases caused by viruses or fungi, for example.

Starter ideas

1 Getting started (10–15 minutes)

Resources: Learner's Book

Description: Ask learners to look at the picture and read the questions in the Learner's Book.

Learners should use their own life experiences and prior knowledge from Stage 4 about infectious diseases to answer the questions.

Use the 'Think-pair-share' method to allow learners to think about their answers for a minute or two, then discuss their answers with a partner before sharing their answers with the class.

2 Brainstorm: how to prevent infectious diseases (10–15 minutes)

Description: Recap with the class what an infectious disease is – a disease that is caused by a living thing (germ) that enters the body and makes you ill.

Have a group brainstorm session for learners to give their ideas of how we can prevent infectious diseases. Write their answers on the board. Learners may mention vaccinations, which they learnt about in Stage 4. Other answers may include washing hands, cooking food properly, not coughing or sneezing over others. You could mention the importance of washing hands in preventing the spread of diseases such as Ebola and Covid-19, which learners will probably have heard of.

If learners do not mention using antibacterial soaps and cleaning products, you can ask them why people use these products. Answers will show whether any learners have the misconception referred to above.

Learners could finish by acting out the modelling exercise from Worksheet 1.4, which shows what happens if there are no measures to prevent diseases spreading.

Main teaching ideas

1 Questions about living things that cause diseases (10–15 minutes; allow an additional 30–40 minutes if you invite an outside speaker to your lesson.)

Learning intention: To find out about living things that cause diseases.

Resources: Learner's Book

> **Digital classroom:** Video: Living things that cause disease (optional). Alternatively, search the internet for images you can use, using terms such as 'cholera bacteria', 'flu virus', 'ringworm fungus' and 'malaria parasite'.

Description: Discuss the different types of living things that cause diseases.

> **Digital classroom:** If you have access to the Digital Classroom component, show the video 'Living things that cause disease', which has slides of disease-causing bacteria, viruses, fungi and other parasites. The i button will explain how to use the video.

Alternatively, show images that you have found yourself, such as pictures of the coronavirus that caused the worldwide Covid-19 disease outbreak in 2019 and 2020.

Learners should read the information in the Learner's Book before answering the questions individually.

To address the Science in Context strand in the curriculum, you could ask a health care worker to speak to the class about some common infectious diseases and how to prevent them. Follow up with a short class discussion about what they learnt from the talk. Check first that you have permission to invite an outside person into your classroom.

> **Differentiation ideas:** Ask more confident learners to think of any infectious disease they have had or know of. Get them to look up information on the type of living thing that causes the disease and how the disease is spread.

They could also attempt Activity 1 in the Learner's Book, which focuses on malaria and dysentery.

> **Assessment ideas:** Discuss answers in class and allow learners to check their own work.

2 Think like a scientist: Analyse hygiene methods that people use (20–30 minutes)

Learning intention: To draw a dot plot of results.

To find out about things we can do to prevent diseases from spreading.

Resources: Learner's Book

Description: In this activity, learners will practise their graphing skills. They should work in pairs to follow the instructions in the Learner's Book.

If you need to revise how to draw a dot plot, refer to the 'New science skills' section at the end of the Stage 4 Learner's Book.

> **Differentiation ideas:** Allow learners with weaker graphing skills to work with a learner who is more proficient at drawing graphs and can give support and assistance.

More confident learners can attempt Question 6.

> **Assessment ideas:** Pairs can answer the questions in the 'How are we doing?' feature in the Learner's Book.

3 Make a poster to show how to prevent diseases spread by insects (60 minutes of class time, plus preparation time at home)

Learning intentions: To find out about things we can do to prevent diseases from spreading.

Resources: Card, coloured pencils, felt tip pens, pictures from magazines, glue, scissors

Description: Learners should make a poster to illustrate and explain four ways we can prevent diseases spreading by insect bites.

The poster should include pictures or drawings and an explanation of why we need to do these things.

You can tell learners in advance to prepare for the activity by looking for pictures from magazines or from the internet for the posters. They could also choose to make their own drawings.

Learners should work in pairs. They should display their posters in class and be able to explain them to other learners.

> **Practical guidance:** Remind learners that they should work carefully if they are using scissors to cut out pictures.

> **Differentiation ideas:** Less confident learners can choose four of the methods described in the Learner's Book.

More confident learners can research additional information. For example:

- sleep under bed nets
- wear long sleeves and long pants
- keep doors and windows closed at night when mosquitoes are active
- use insect repellents on your skin to keep insects away
- burn mosquito coils to keep insects away
- remove any standing water in or around your home as insects such as mosquitoes breed in still water
- wear light-coloured clothing outdoors

> **Assessment ideas:** Ask learners to look at other groups' posters and use this checklist of questions to assess them. They can rate the posters by drawing four stars next to the question if they think that aspect of the poster is very good, three stars if the work is good, two stars if it is okay and one star if it is not good:

	★★★★
Does the poster show four ways to prevent insect bites?	
Does the poster explain why we need to prevent insect bites?	
Is the written information easy to read and understand?	
Does the poster look good?	

Plenary ideas

1 Wordsearch (5–10 minutes)

Resources: Unit 1 wordsearch template:

Q	W	E	B	R	U	T	R
P	A	R	A	S	I	T	E
A	S	D	R	G	H	L	P
F	E	R	R	V	U	D	E
H	Y	G	I	E	N	E	L
O	S	V	E	C	B	F	L
S	O	P	R	T	M	E	E
T	X	N	V	O	U	N	N
D	H	O	E	R	C	C	T
S	M	U	C	U	S	E	Y

Clues:

1   A living thing that lives on or in the body of another living thing
2   A living thing that a parasite infects
3   Protection against something
4   An object that stops things getting through or past it, for example a fence or a gate
5   Sticky substance found in our noses, windpipe and other air passages
6   Keeping yourself and the things around you clean
7   A living thing that spreads diseases but does not cause it
8   A substance that keeps insects away

Description: The wordsearch contains key words learnt in the topic. Learners should use the clues to find the words and circle the word or shade in the letters.

Make a copy of the word search grid and clues for each learner.

Answers

Q	W	E	B	R	U	T	R
P	A	R	A	S	I	T	E
A	S	D	R	G	H	L	P
F	E	R	R	V	U	D	E
H	Y	G	I	E	N	E	L
O	S	V	E	C	B	F	L
S	O	P	R	T	M	E	E
T	X	N	V	O	U	N	N
D	H	O	E	R	C	C	T
S	M	U	C	U	S	E	Y

parasite: a living thing that lives on or in the body of another living thing

host: a living thing that a parasite infects

defence: protection against something

barrier: an object that stops things getting through or past it, for example a fence or a gate

mucus: sticky substance found in our noses, windpipe and other air passages

hygiene: keeping yourself and the things around you clean

vector: a living thing that spreads diseases but does not cause it

repellent: a substance that keeps insects away

> **Assessment ideas:** Learners can swap grids with one another. Project the wordsearch grid with answers circled or highlighted words for learners to check one another's work. Ask learners to state the meaning of each of the words as you point to them on the grid.

> **Reflection ideas:** Ask learners:

• Was it easy to find the words in the wordsearch?
• Were there any words you did not know the meaning of?
• Were there any words you did not know how to spell?

2 I can and I know (5 minutes)

Resources: Paper and pens or pencils

Description: Ask learners to each write down three sentences about what they have learnt in the topic. Their sentences should start with either:

I can…

or

I know…

Give learners one or two minutes to write their sentences. Then write or project a list of success criteria onto the board. Learners can compare their sentences with the success criteria to assess if they have grasped the main ideas and skills covered in the topic.

> **Assessment ideas:** This is a self-assessment activity which will help learners to identify areas where they are succeeding or where they need more support.

> **Reflection ideas:** Learners can answer the Reflection questions in the Learner's Book.

CROSS-CURRICULAR LINKS

Drawing a dot plot from data given in Main teaching idea 2 links with data handling and graphing in Maths.

Designing and making a poster in Main teaching idea 3 links with Arts and crafts.

The wordsearch exercise suggested for Plenary idea 2 can assist with vocabulary development in English.

Homework ideas

1   Learners could make a collage with pictures or drawings of different things we can do at home to help prevent the spread of diseases. In the next lesson, let learners display their collages and look at one another's work to assess how well they think they have completed the task.

2   Learners can complete Activity 2 in the Learner's Book.

   In the next lesson, discuss answers in class. Allow learners swap answers and check each other's work.

Topic Worksheet

Worksheet 1.4: Model the spread of a disease

The worksheet activity is a simulation of how diseases spread if there are no measures to prevent them and, conversely, how preventative measures such as good hygiene, can limit the spread of a disease. It is recommended that you try to do the worksheet activity in a larger space than a classroom, such as in a hall or outdoors. It is a whole-class activity which should take about 40 minutes to complete.

There is a Help sheet to support learners who need more background on the spread of diseases and Stretch questions for more confident learners.

PROJECT: THE CIRCULATORY SYSTEM

Learning objectives

6SIC.01 Describe how scientific knowledge and understanding changes over time through the use of evidence gained by enquiry.

6TWSc.07 Use a range of secondary information sources to research and select relevant evidence to answer questions.

Part 1

Learners should work individually to read the information about the scientific understanding of the circulatory system and answer the questions that follow.

Learners should work in pairs to draw their timelines.

Part 2

Learners should work in pairs to draw their timelines.

Assessment rubric

You can use this rubric to assess learners' timelines.

Assessment criteria	Level 1	Level 2	Level 3	Level 4
Timeline title	No title given	Incomplete title or unsuitable title	Suitable title	Suitable and creative title
New information researched	Not done	Some information wrong or missing	Mostly complete and correct	All complete and correct
Information presented	Information for few or no events/ discoveries correct	Information for some events/ discoveries correct	Information for most events/ discoveries correct	Information for all events/ discoveries correct
Accuracy	Only 1 or 2 dates are correct and in the proper order	3–5 dates are correct and in the proper order	Most dates are correct and in the proper order	All dates are correct and in the proper order
Appearance	Untidy and poorly organised

Little or no use of colours or pictures to enhance appearance | Some attempt to be organised and neat

Some use of colours or pictures to enhance appearance | Organised, neat and clear

Good use of colours or pictures to enhance appearance | Well organised, neat, easy to read

Very good use of colours or pictures to enhance appearance |

> 2 Materials: properties and changes

Unit plan

Topic	Approx. number of learning hours	Outline of learning content	Resources
2.1 Properties of substances	2.5–3	• Melting and boiling points as properties of substances; difference between boiling and evaporation; properties of gases.	**Learner's Book:** Activity: Compare boiling and evaporation Think like a scientist 1: Measure and compare melting points Think like a scientist 2: Plan a test to compare boiling points of substances Think like a scientist 3: Investigate the properties of gases **Workbook:** Topic 2.1 ⤓ Worksheet 2.1.1 ⤓ Worksheet 2.1.2A, 2.1.2B, 2.1.2C
2.2 Thermal and electrical conductors	3–3.5	• Conduction of heat and electricity as properties of substances.	**Learner's Book:** Think like a scientist 1: Investigate how well different materials conduct heat Think like a scientist 2: Investigate how well different substances conduct electricity Activity: Compare thermal and electrical conductors **Workbook:** Topic 2.2
2.3 Reversible changes	3–3.5	• Reversible physical changes, effect of temperature on dissolving.	**Learner's Book:** Think like a scientist 1: Demonstrate a reversible change Activity: Describe dissolving Think like a scientist 2: Does water temperature affect the rate of dissolving? Think like a scientist 3: Ask and investigate a question about dissolving **Workbook:** Topic 2.3 ⤓ Worksheet 2.3 **Digital Classroom:** Video – Reversible and irreversible changes

Topic	Approx. number of learning hours	Outline of learning content	Resources
2.4 Chemical reactions	2–2.5	• Reactants and products in chemical reactions; evidence for chemical reactions.	**Learner's Book:** Think like a scientist 1: Identify reactants and products Think like a scientist 2: Investigate evidence for chemical reactions A and Investigate evidence for chemical reactions B **Workbook:** Topic 2.4 ⬇ Worksheet 2.4 **Digital Classroom:** Video – Chemical reactions

Across unit resources		
Learner's Book: Project: Electrical insulators Check your progress quiz	**Teacher's Book:** ⬇ Language worksheets 1 & 2 ⬇ Diagnostic test ⬇ Mid-year test ⬇ End-of-year test ⬇ End-of-unit test	**Digital Classroom:** End-of-unit quiz

BACKGROUND KNOWLEDGE

Properties of substances

All substances have properties that we can use to identify them. The properties can be either physical or chemical. The physical properties of a substance can be observed and measured, and if those properties change, there is no change to the chemical makeup or nature of the substance. Colour, smell, boiling point, melting point, magnetic attraction or repulsion are examples of physical properties. The ability to conduct heat or electricity are also physical properties of substances. Chemical properties allow a substance to change into a new substance and describe how a substance reacts with another substance. For example, the way a substance reacts when it is mixed with an acid is a chemical property of the substance. We can only measure or observe chemical properties when we change the chemical makeup or nature of a substance.

Reversible changes

A reversible change is a physical change to a substance or material that can be undone or reversed. It changes how a material or substance looks or feels, but it doesn't form a new material or

substance as there is no change to the particles of the substances or materials themselves. Changes of state, such as melting and boiling, are reversible changes. In a reversible change, the substances before and after the change are the same, even though they may look different, for example, melted candle wax does not look the same as the solid wax in the candle, but it is still the same substance.

Chemical reactions

Chemical reactions involve changes to the arrangement of particles or molecules in substances. These changes are irreversible. In a chemical reaction, substances called reactants combine to form new substances called products. Evidence that a chemical reaction has taken place includes light, heat, colour change, gas production, smell or sound. Examples of chemical changes include combustion (burning), mixing plaster of Paris with water, cooking an egg, rusting of an iron nail. When plaster of Paris is mixed with water it gives off heat which shows it is a chemical change. Learners will investigate and observe the formation of a gas and changes in colour and temperature as evidence of chemical reactions.

TEACHING SKILLS FOCUS

Peer assessment and feedback

Peer assessment occurs when learners assess each other's work in a summative way. That is, they provide each other with a grade or qualitative assessment of how good they think their peers' work is. For example, ticking a checklist to say if they think their peers' work was good, okay or not good is a form of qualitative assessment.

Peer feedback is not the same as peer assessment. Peer feedback occurs when learners make suggestions or give each other advice about how to improve their work. It includes explaining the following to one another:

- what has been done well in relation to the success criteria. For example, identifying the effect of temperature on dissolving.
- what still needs to be done in order to achieve the success criteria. For example, the learner needs to explain why the sugar dissolved faster when the solution was heated.
- advice on how to achieve that improvement. For example, suggesting the learner thinks about what happens to the particles of a substance when we heat the substance.

Peer feedback is a useful strategy for learners to think about their knowledge and understanding in order to give feedback to others. For peer feedback to be effective, learners need to feel comfortable with each other and feel able to take risks and make mistakes. Learners also need to respect each other's opinions. Teachers will need to create an environment in which risk-taking is accepted and there are no 'put-downs' from other learners when a learner makes a mistake.

Here are some ideas for peer feedback strategies:

Two stars and a wish – learners identify two positive things (the 'stars') about their peers' work and a 'wish' about what could be done better. For example, a star for identifying the effect of temperature on dissolving, a star for drawing and labeling the solution, and a wish that the learner explains more clearly why their test was fair.

Traffic lights – learners can show a green card or use a green sticker to show another learner if they have met all the success criteria, for example identifying examples of chemical reactions. Learners use a yellow card or sticker if some of the success criteria have been met, and a red card or sticker if the success criteria are not met. Learners should then explain to their peers why or how the success criteria were not met.

Rubrics – a rubric helps learners to know what aspects they need to focus on when reflecting on their peers' work. A rubric will also help them understand how the success criteria should be met so they can give feedback based on those standards. Challenge yourself to try a peer feedback strategy at least once in every topic of the unit.

2.1 Materials: properties and changes

LEARNING PLAN

Learning objectives	Learning intentions	Success criteria
6Cp.01 Know that the temperature at which a substance changes state is a property of the substance.	- To learn that the temperature at which a substance changes state is a property of the substance.	- Learners can understand that the temperature at which a substance changes state is a property of the substance.
6Cc.03 Describe the difference between boiling and evaporation.	- To learn about the difference between boiling and evaporation.	- Learners can describe the difference between boiling and evaporation.

CONTINUED

Learning objectives	Learning intentions	Success criteria
6Cp.02 Know that gases have properties, including mass.	• To find out about the properties of gases.	• Learners can identify properties of gases.
6TWSc.05 Take appropriately accurate measurements.	• To measure temperature.	• Learners can measure temperature.
6TWSc.08 Collect and record observations and/or measurements in tables and diagrams appropriate to the type of scientific enquiry.	• To collect and record observations and measurements in tables.	• Learners can collect and record observations and measurements in tables.
6TWSc.06 Carry out practical work safely.	• To work safely in practical investigations.	• Learners can work safely in practical investigations.
6TWSa.05 Present and interpret results using tables, bar charts, dot plots, line graphs and scatter graphs.	• To draw graphs of results and measurements.	• Learners can draw graphs of results and measurements.
6TWSa.03 Make a conclusion from results informed by scientific understandings.	• To make conclusions from results and measurements.	• Learners can make conclusions from results and measurements.
6TWSp.04 Plan fair test investigations, identifying the independent, dependent and control variables.	• To plan a fair test.	• Learners can plan a fair test.
6TWSc.03 Choose equipment to carry out an investigation and use it appropriately.	• To choose materials and equipment to use.	• Learners can choose materials and equipment to use.
6TWSp.05 Describe risks when planning practical work and consider how to minimise them.	• To identify risks and how to work safely when planning a practical investigation.	• Learners can identify risks and how to work safely when planning a practical investigation.
6TWSp.03 Make predictions, referring to relevant scientific knowledge and understanding within familiar and unfamiliar contexts.	• To use scientific knowledge to make a prediction.	• Learners can use scientific knowledge to make a prediction.
6TWSa.01 Describe the accuracy of predictions, based on results.	• To use results to say if a prediction was accurate.	• Learners can use results to say if a prediction was accurate.

LANGUAGE SUPPORT

Learners will use the following words:

melting point: the temperature at which a solid becomes a liquid

property: something about a substance that allows us to tell it apart from other substances. For example, liquids take the shape of the container they are in is a property of liquids. Explain that the term 'property' has other meanings. For example,

something that belongs to you is your property; a piece of land or a building is also called property

boiling point: the temperature at which particles throughout a liquid become a gas

Give learners the opportunity to use these words correctly by letting them explain the terms to a partner.

Common misconceptions

Misconception	How to identify	How to overcome
Gases have no mass.	Blow up a balloon. Ask learners to say what is inside the balloon (air/gas). Ask if the mass of the balloon changes when it is full of air.	Carry out Think like a scientist 3 activity.
The temperature of a boiling liquid increases over time if the liquid continues boiling.	Boil some water and measure its temperature. Ask learners to predict the temperature of the water if it boils for three minutes.	Measure the water temperature after it boils for three minutes. Learners will see that the temperature has not changed. This is because the temperature is the boiling point of water which is one of its properties.

Starter ideas

1 Getting started (10–15 minutes)

Resources: Learner's Book

Description: This activity draws on learners' existing knowledge about change of state.

Tell learners to work in groups to brainstorm what they know about change of state. They should share three things from their mind map with another group. Groups can use the 'Two stars and a wish' strategy to give feedback to their peers about their ideas.

2 Change of state True or False? (5–10 minutes)

Description: Ask learners to decide if each of the suggested statements about change of state is true or false.

- Substances change state when they are heated and cooled. (T)
- Freezing and solidifying are the same process. (T)
- Boiling and evaporation are the same process. (F)

- When ice melts, it forms a new substance. (F)
- A gas can condense to form a liquid. (T)
- Ice melts because its particles lose energy. (F)

Learners can indicate their answers by a show of hands. Take note of any learners who give incorrect answers. Follow up with these learners to find out which aspects of change of state they do not understand and give support as needed.

Main teaching ideas

1 Think like a scientist 1: Measure and compare melting points (50–60 minutes)

Learning intentions: To learn that the temperature at which a substance changes state is a property of the substance.

To measure temperature.

To collect and record observations and measurements in tables.

To draw graphs of results and measurements.

To make conclusions from results and measurements.

Resources: Learner's Book; Worksheet 2.1.1 (optional)

Per group: three different solids, three pans, a hotplate, a thermometer, a stopwatch, timer or digital watch

Description: A teacher demonstration, as described in 'Practical guidance', is recommended.

Learners should observe that each substance has a different melting point.

As consolidation, learners should answer the questions in the Learner's Book.

Learners could also complete Worksheet 2.1.1

> **Practical guidance:** Solids used could include ice, butter, candle wax, beeswax, soap and coconut oil.

Make sure all learners can see what is happening. You could ask learners to volunteer to measure the melting point temperature of each substance. Remind learners how to measure temperature if needed. Record these measurements on the board for learners to use for drawing their graphs.

> **Differentiation ideas:** More confident learners could answer questions 4 and 5 from the Learner's Book.

2 **Think like a scientist 2: Plan a test to compare boiling points of substances (20 minutes)**

Learning intentions: To plan a fair test.

To choose materials and equipment to use.

To identify risks and how to work safely when planning a practical investigation .

Resources: Learner's Book, Worksheets 2.1.2A, 2.1.2B and 2.1.2C (optional)

Description: Tell learners to read the instructions in the Learner's Book.

They should be able to apply their understanding of fair testing to plan a test similar to the test in Think like a scientist 1 to compare boiling points of different liquids.

Learners could finish by completing Worksheet 2.1.2A, B or C which describe the results from investigating boiling.

> **Practical guidance:** Divide learners into groups of 4–5.

Allow about 15 minutes planning time. Ask the groups to show their plans to you. Guide them if their plans do not seem suitable.

> **Differentiation ideas:** Recap on the role of dependent, independent and control variables in a fair test investigation for learners you feel will need

help with this.

Group learners in mixed-ability groups so that less confident learners can be encouraged and helped by more confident learners.

Learners who need more support should be given Worksheet 2.1.2A and more confident learners should be given Worksheet 2.1.2C, if using these as part of the activity.

> **Assessment ideas:** Learners can answer the self-assessment questions in the 'How am I doing?' feature in the Learner's Book.

3 **Demonstrate that gases have mass (10–15 minutes)**

Learning intentions: To find out about the properties of gases.

Resources: Balloon, electronic balance or scale

You can also do an internet search for videos that show that a gas has mass.

Description: This activity is a teacher demonstration which will show learners that a gas has mass.

> **Practical guidance:** Place the deflated balloon on the balance and measure its mass. Write the reading on the board.

Blow up the balloon and tie it off at the neck so no air escapes. Ask the learners what is inside the balloon (air/gas).

Ask learners to predict the mass of the inflated balloon. Their answers will help you identify the misconception that gases have no mass.

Measure the mass of the balloon again. The measurement shows the gas in the balloon has mass.

> **Differentiation ideas:** If some learners seem to have difficulty in grasping the concept that gases have mass, you can ask these questions:

Why did the balloon get bigger when you blew air into it? (The air filled up the balloon – this shows understanding that gases take up space.)

Was the mass of the balloon the same after it was blown up? (No).

Explain that, if a gas had no mass, then the mass of the balloon would stay the same so, the gas in the balloon must have mass.

> **Assessment ideas:** Learners can explain to a partner how the demonstration showed them that gases have mass. The partner can use the 'Two stars and a wish' strategy to give feedback.

Plenary ideas

1 What have you learnt? (5 minutes)

Description: Let learners stand and quickly say one thing that they have learnt in the topic before sitting down. You will probably not have time for all learners to give an answer, so ask five or six learners to volunteer their ideas.

〉 **Assessment ideas:** Learners' answers should give you a quick overview of how well the class has understood the work covered in the topic.

2 Traffic lights (10–15 minutes)

Resources: Teacher focus for this unit

Per pair: a red, a green and yellow card or sticker

Description: Learners should work in pairs to give one another feedback on whether they have met the following success criteria for the topic:

- can describe the difference between boiling and evaporation
- can say why the temperature at which a substance changes state is a property of the substance
- can say how they know that gases have mass and take up space
- can identify the different variables when planning a fair test

Learners should show the green card if all the success criteria are met, the yellow card if some are met and the red card if none are met.

〉 **Reflection ideas:** Learners can answer the Reflection questions at the end of the topic in the Learner's Book.

CROSS-CURRICULAR LINKS

Recording data in a table and drawing a graph in Main teaching idea 1 links with data handling and graphing in Maths.

Writing answers to questions throughout the topic can be linked with sentence construction and vocabulary development in English.

Homework ideas

1. Learners could complete the Focus, Practice or Challenge Exercises for the topic in the Workbook, depending on their progress.

   In the next lesson, discuss answers. Learners can check their own answers.

2. Learners can make a table to compare the differences between evaporation and boiling.

   In the next lesson, discuss answers. Learners can work in pairs to check one another's answers using the traffic light method discussed previously.

Topic Worksheets

Worksheet 2.1 Materials: Properties and changes

Worksheet 2.1.1 consolidates learners' understanding of melting point as a property of a substance and provides practice in drawing line graphs. The Help sheet will support learners who need support to know the most appropriate type of graph to draw from the data given. Stretch questions 3 and 4 are aimed at more confident learners.

Worksheets 2.1.2A, B and C give learners additional practice in drawing and interpreting line graphs. All learners should be able to complete worksheet 2.1.2A. Most learners should be able to complete Worksheet 2.1.2B. More confident learners can attempt Worksheet 2.1.2C.

2.2 Thermal and electrical conductors

LEARNING PLAN

Learning objectives	Learning intentions	Success criteria
6Cp.03 Understand that electrical conductivity and thermal conductivity are properties of a substance.	• To learn that conducting heat and electricity are properties of a substance.	• Learners can understand that conducting heat and electricity are properties of a substance.
6TWSp.02 Know the features of the five main types of scientific enquiry.	• To identify the type/s of scientific enquiry used in an investigation.	• Learners can identify the type/s of scientific enquiry used in an investigation.
6TWSp.03 Make predictions, referring to relevant scientific knowledge and understanding within familiar and unfamiliar contexts.	• To use scientific knowledge to make a prediction.	• Learners can use scientific knowledge to make a prediction.
6TWSa.01 Describe the accuracy of predictions, based on results.	• To use results to say if a prediction was accurate.	• Learners can use results to say if a prediction was accurate.
6TWSc.04 Decide when observations and measurements need to be repeated to give more reliable data.	• To decide when measurements should be repeated.	• Learners can decide when measurements should be repeated.
6TWSc.08 Collect and record observations and/or measurements in tables and diagrams appropriate to the type of scientific enquiry.	• To collect and record observations and measurements in tables.	• Learners can collect and record observations and measurements in tables.
6TWSa.05 Present and interpret results using tables, bar charts, dot plots, line graphs and scatter graphs.	• To draw a graph of results and measurements.	• Learners can draw a graph of results and measurements.
6TWSa.02 Describe patterns in results, including identifying any anomalous results.	• To identify and describe a pattern in results.	• Learners can identify and describe a pattern in results.
6TWSc.06 Carry out practical work safely.	• To work safely in practical investigations.	• Learners can work safely in practical investigations.
6TWSa.03 Make a conclusion from results informed by scientific understanding.	• To make conclusions from results and measurements.	• Learners can make conclusions from results and measurements.

CONTINUED

Learning objectives	Learning intentions	Success criteria
6TWSa.04 Suggest how an investigation could be improved and explain any proposed changes.	• To suggest how to improve an investigation.	• Learners can suggest how to improve an investigation.
6TWSc.01 Sort, group and classify objects, materials and living things through testing, observation and using secondary information.	• To group substances according to their properties.	• Learners can group substances according to their properties.

LANGUAGE SUPPORT

The key terms for this topic are:

conduction: the transfer of heat energy from one object to another

thermal conductors: materials and substances that conduct heat well

electrical conductors: materials and substances that conduct electricity well

Explain that we use the word 'conductor' in other ways in our everyday life. For example, an orchestra or choir has a conductor who stands in front of the players or singers and directs their playing or singing. A conductor on a bus or train checks passengers' tickets or collects ticket money from people.

Starter ideas

1 Getting started (5–10 minutes)

Resources: Learner's Book

Description: This activity draws on learners' existing knowledge about transfer of heat energy by conduction.

Tell learners to read the instructions in the Learner's Book.

Learners should work in pairs to draw their energy chains and then explain their energy chain to another group.

2 Which materials conduct electricity? (10–15 minutes)

Resources: The classroom

Description: This activity draws on prior knowledge about materials that are electrical conductors and insulators. Learners should work individually to identify electrical conductors and insulators in the classroom. Ask these questions:

- Which materials can conduct electricity? (E.g. metal, water.)
- Which materials cannot conduct electricity? (E.g. paper, wood.)

Learners should then test a partner. Learners name three materials and ask their partner if the materials conduct electricity or not. They should then swap roles.

Main teaching ideas

1 Think like a scientist 1: Investigate how well different materials conduct heat (30–40 minutes)

Learning intention: To learn that conducting heat and electricity are properties of a substance.

To use scientific knowledge to make a prediction.

To use results to say if a prediction was accurate.

To work safely in practical investigations.

To collect and record observations and measurements in tables.

To suggest how to improve an investigation.

To make conclusions from results and measurements.

To identify the type/s of scientific enquiry used in an investigation.

Resources: Learner's Book

A beaker of hot water, a metal teaspoon, a plastic teaspoon, a glass rod, a pencil, a piece of polystyrene, five beads, petroleum jelly

Description: Read through the instructions in the Learner's Book with the class to make sure learners know what to do. This can be a learner-led investigation, or you can set it up as a demonstration if you have concerns about learners working with hot water.

If learners do the activity themselves, make sure they are aware of the danger of working with hot water. You should pour the water into the beakers for the learner groups.

Learners will be observing changes over time in the investigation and carrying out a fair test.

⟩ **Practical guidance:** It should take few minutes for the beads to start falling off the spoons, depending on how hot the water is. Learners should note the order in which the beads fall off the spoons. They should observe that the bead falls off the metal spoon first.

⟩ **Differentiation ideas:** Challenge more confident learners to investigate if some metals conduct heat better than others. They could test different types of metal wire, for example lengths of copper wire, brass wire and steel wire.

Learners can answer the self-assessment questions from the 'How am I doing? feature in the Learner's Book.

2 **Think like a scientist 2: Investigate how well different substances conduct electricity (40–50 minutes)**

Learning intentions: To learn that conducting heat and electricity are properties of a substance.

To use scientific knowledge to make a prediction.

To use results to say if a prediction was accurate.

To collect and record observations and measurements in tables.

To make conclusions from results and measurements.

To group substances according to their properties.

Resources: Learner's Book

Per group: two cells, a cell holder, a 1.5 V lamp, three 15 cm pieces of connecting wire, a steel paper clip, aluminium foil, a beaker of tap water, sugar, pencil graphite

Description: In this investigation, learners will test how well different substances conduct electricity. Discuss the components of the circuit shown in the Learner's Book and check that learners are able to set it up for themselves. Let learners read through the instructions to make sure they know what to do.

Learners will do the test only once. Discuss what we mean by reliable results – results that will be the same or similar if we do the test over again. Remind them that scientists always check their results.

To link with the Science in Context strand of the curriculum, ask learners to look out for the use of electrical conductors around them at home or in their local area. They could take photos of these with mobile phones if they have them. In the next lesson discuss the examples learners have found. These could include electricity pylons and overhead electric cables, the metal pins on electrical plugs, the metal filaments in electric lamps (light bulbs), jumper cables to start cars with flat batteries, and the metal terminals at the ends of cells/batteries.

⟩ **Practical guidance:** Learners should work in groups of 4 or 5, depending on how many circuits you have components for.

Prepare lengths of wire about 20 cm long. Strip off about 2 cm of plastic insulation from the ends of each length of wire.

If you have access to an ammeter or multimeter, you can measure the current in the circuit for each of the substances tested. This will give you a numerical value for the relative ability of each substance to conduct electricity. The reading in amps on the meter will be higher for good conductors.

To obtain graphite, either sharpen a pencil at both ends or use the 'lead' from a from mechanical/propelling pencil.

⟩ **Differentiation ideas:** Group learners in mixed ability groups so that less confident learners can be encouraged and helped by more confident learners.

3 Activity: Compare thermal and electrical conductors (15–20 minutes)

Learning intentions: To learn that conducting heat and electricity are properties of a substance.

To draw graphs of results and measurements.

To make conclusions from results and measurements.

To group substances according to their properties.

Resources: Learner's Book

Description: In this activity, learners use a table of measurements given in the Learner's Book to draw a scatter graph which shows that substances that are good thermal conductors are also good electrical conductors. Learners should work on their own for the activity. It is not necessary at this level to include the units in which electrical and thermal conductivity are measured. Learners should focus on the numerical values in the table.

> **Differentiation ideas:** Demonstrate how to draw a scatter graph to support learners who still need to master this skill. Also refer to the Skills section at the end of the Learner's Book.

More confident learners could answer question 5.

> **Assessment ideas:** You could use this checklist to assess learners' answers.

Assessment criteria	Well	Quite well	Needed help
How well did the learners …			
draw a scatter graph of the measurements?			
identify and describe a pattern in the data?			
use the data and graph to identify the best and worst conductors of heat and electricity?			
use the graph to predict and graph the heat conduction value of another substance?			

Plenary ideas

1 I can and I know (5–10 minutes}

Resources: Paper and pens or pencils

Description: Ask learners to each write two sentences about what they have learnt in the topic. Their sentences should start with either:

I can …
or
I know …

Give learners one or two minutes to write their sentences. Then write or project a list of success criteria onto the board. Learners can compare their sentences with the success criteria to assess if they have grasped the main ideas and skills covered in the topic.

> **Assessment ideas:** This is a self-assessment activity which will help learners to identify areas where they are succeeding or where they need more support.

> **Reflection ideas:** Ask learners:

What things did you find easy to learn?

What did you find difficult?

How did you deal with the difficult things?

What would you like to know more about?

2 Talk about it (10–15 minutes)

Resources: A piece of work the learners have completed in the topic

Description: Learners should think about what they did well in the piece of work and how they think they can improve on it.

> **Assessment ideas:** Learners can give each other feedback on their work using the 'two stars and a wish' method.

> **Reflection ideas:** Learners can answer the Reflection questions in the Learner's Book.

CROSS-CURRICULAR LINKS

Drawing a graph in Main teaching idea 3 links with graphing in Maths.

Reading, following written instructions and writing answer sentences can be linked with comprehension skills and sentence construction in English.

Homework idea 2 can be linked with ICT skills.

Homework ideas

1 Learners could complete the Focus, Practice and/or Challenge Exercises of the Workbook, depending on their progress.

In the next lesson, discuss answers. Learners can work in pairs to check one another's answers.

2 Learners could do some research to find out why we need lightning conductors, what they are made of and how they work. In the next lesson, ask four or five volunteers to share one thing they have found out. Write their ideas on the board to make a mind map for the class about lighting conductors.

2.3 Reversible changes

LEARNING PLAN

Learning objectives	Learning intentions	Success criteria
6Cc.01 Identify and describe physical changes that are reversible.	• To find out about and describe changes to substances that are reversible.	• Learners can understand and describe changes to substances that are reversible.
6Cc.02 Describe how temperature affects solids dissolving in liquids and relate it to the particle model.	• To use the particle model to explain how temperature affects dissolving.	• Learners can use the particle model to explain how temperature affects dissolving.
6TWSp.03 Make predictions, referring to relevant scientific knowledge and understanding within familiar and unfamiliar contexts.	• To use scientific knowledge to make a prediction.	• Learners can use scientific knowledge to make a prediction.
6TWSa.01 Describe the accuracy of predictions, based on results.	• To use results to say if a prediction was accurate.	• Learners can use results to say if a prediction was accurate.
6TWSc.08 Collect and record observations and/or measurements in tables and diagrams appropriate to the type of scientific enquiry.	• To collect and record results in a table.	• Learners can collect and record results in a table.
6TWSc.03 Choose equipment to carry out an investigation and use it appropriately.	• To choose materials and equipment to use.	• Learners can choose materials and equipment to use.
6TWSp.05 Describe risks when planning practical work and consider how to minimise them.	• To identify risks and how to work safely in practical work.	• Learners can identify risks and how to work safely in practical work.
6TWSa.02 Describe patterns in results, including identifying any anomalous results.	• To identify and describe a pattern in results.	• Learners can identify and describe a pattern in results.
6TWSc.06 Carry out practical work safely.	• To work safely in practical investigations.	• Learners can work safely in practical investigations.
6TWSa.03 Make a conclusion from results informed by scientific understanding.	• To make conclusions from results and measurements.	• Learners can make conclusions from results and measurements.

LEARNING PLAN CONTINUED

Learning objectives	Learning intentions	Success criteria
6TWSp.04 Plan fair test investigations, identifying the independent, dependent and control variables.	• To decide if a test is fair.	• Learners can decide if a test is fair.
6TWSp.01 Ask scientific questions and select appropriate scientific enquiries to use.	• To ask a question to investigate and choose a type of scientific enquiry to find the answer.	• Learners can ask a question to investigate and choose a type of scientific enquiry to find the answer.
6TWSp.02 Know the features of the five main types of scientific enquiry.	• To ask a question to investigate and choose a type of scientific enquiry to find the answer.	• Learners can ask a question to investigate and choose a type of scientific enquiry to find the answer.

LANGUAGE SUPPORT

The key terms for this topic are:

reversible: can be changed back to the way it was before. For example, making a lump of clay into a shape is reversible because it can be made back into a lump. The word 'reversible' can also be used to describe something like an item of clothing that has been designed so that either side of it can be worn on the inside or outside, such as a reversible coat.

irreversible: cannot be changed back to the way it was before. For example, burning a piece of wood is irreversible

physical change: any change that does not change a substance into a different substance, for example, melting

solute: the solid in a solution

solvent: the liquid in a solution

uniform: the same throughout; a uniform is also a set of clothing that people wear to do identify them as going to a certain school, or working for a particular business or doing a certain job, for example a nurse's or police officer's uniform.

rate: how fast something happens, for example our rate of breathing is the number of times we breathe in and out in a minute

Where possible, use familiar examples or contexts to explain the words. For example, the term 'uniform'.

Ask learners to explain to one another the difference between pairs of related terms, for example, solute and solvent and reversible and irreversible.

Common misconceptions

Misconception	How to identify	How to overcome
Dissolving is not a physical change.	Make a solution of water and salt. Ask the class if any of the substances have changed. Is the water still water, or is it something else? Is salt still salt? Ask learners if we can separate the salt and the water or if they have formed new substance.	Learners should recall how to separate salt and water from Stage 5. Explain that in most physical changes we can get back the substances we started with. The substances may look a bit different, but their particles have not changed in any way, expect possibly in their arrangement. You can use the example of building blocks. We can arrange them in different ways to make structures that look different, but the actual blocks in each structure do not change.

Starter ideas

1 Getting started (15–20 minutes)

Resources: Learner's Book, ice cubes, saucer, watch

Description: This activity recaps on change of state of substances.

Tell learners to read the instructions in the Learner's Book.

Learners should work in groups. Each learner should make his or her own drawing of their observations.

Ask learners to volunteer to explain their observations to the class. Tell them to use the particle model in their explanation.

2 Does a new substance form? (15–20 minutes)

Resources: Digital Classroom: Video: Reversible and irreversible changes (optional), or images from the internet of, for example water boiling, ice cream melting, rusty metal, wood burning, bread/cake baking in an oven, a fizzy tablet dissolving in a glass of water, stirring sugar into tea, condensation on a mirror or drinks can, frozen foods in a freezer, food rotting.

Description

> **Digital Classroom:** If you have access to the Digital Classroom component, show the video 'Reversible and irreversible changes'. The i button will explain how to use the video.

Alternatively, show the images you found from the internet. Ask learners to identify the process shown in each slide, for example melting, burning, rusting, freezing.

Then ask learners in which slides a new substance is formed (rusty metal, wood burning, cake baking in an oven, burnt toast, fizzy tablet dissolving, food rotting). Ask them for reasons for their answers.

You could introduce the terms reversible changes and irreversible changes at this point. Reshow the slide and show learners which slides show reversible changes.

Main teaching ideas

1 Think like a scientist 1: Demonstrate a reversible change (40–50 minutes, plus time overnight if needed)

Learning intention: To find out about and describe changes to substances that are reversible.

Resources: Learner's Book

Materials for each group, such as candles, candle holders, matches, mirrors, butter, coconut oil, chocolate, bowls, water, salt, plastic wrap, elastic bands, laboratory beakers, coloured crystals, burner or hotplate, pan. If you have access to a freezer, you could also put out ice cube trays.

Description: Learners should read the instructions for the activity in the Learner's Book.

They should decide on the reversible change they want to demonstrate and choose the materials and equipment they need.

Explain that not all substances or materials will look the same as they did before the reversible change. For example, if learners melt an ice cube and then refreeze the water into an ice cube, the new ice cube will look the same as the ice cube they melted. If they melt chocolate and then cool the chocolate to change it back to a solid, the solidified chocolate will look different (it will be a different shape and look duller) compared to before it was melted. Learners should be able to grasp that this is still a reversible change because even though the substance is not exactly the same as it was to start with, no new substances were formed during the change.

At the end of the activity ask learners:

- Is the material exactly the same now as it was before you changed it? If not, how is it different?

- If there are differences, is the change you demonstrated really reversible? Why or why not?

To incorporate the Science in Context strand of the curriculum, you could look for a video clip on the internet on how chocolate is made. The final part of the process involves melting and solidifying which are reversible physical changes. Use a search term such as 'how chocolate is made'. If you have a jeweller in the local area, you could try to arrange a class visit for learners to observe how metals are heated until they start to soften and melt. The metal is then shaped and cooled to make pieces of jewellery such as rings and bracelets.

> **Practical guidance:** This a learner-led activity.

Learners should work in groups of 4–5.

Safety: Supervise learners who decide to melt substances or demonstrate boiling over a flame or on a hotplate to ensure that they do not burn themselves.

Changes such as evaporation and freezing or solidifying will take longer to demonstrate than dissolving and melting. Allow these changes to take place overnight.

> **Differentiation ideas:** More confident learners can do some research to find out how reversible changes are used in one of the following processes:

- making chocolate (if you have not already shown a video on this)

- recycling glass

- recycling metal cans.

> **Assessment ideas:** Learners can answer the peer assessment questions in the 'How are we doing?' feature in the Learner's Book.

You can use also this checklist to assess learners' demonstrations:

Were learners able to:	Yes	Needed help	No
identify a reversible change to demonstrate?			
choose which equipment to use?			
use the equipment correctly?			
describe the change?			
explain why the change is reversible?			

2 Think like a scientist 2: Does water temperature affect the rate of dissolving? (20–30 minutes)

Learning intention: To use the particle model to explain how temperature affects dissolving.

To use scientific knowledge to make a prediction.

To use results to say if a prediction was accurate.

To collect and record observations and measurements in tables.

To decide if a test is fair.

To make a conclusion from results and measurements.

Resources: Learner's Book

Per group: sugar, two glass jars or beakers, cold water, hot water, a teaspoon, a measuring cylinder, a stopwatch or timer

Description: Learners often confuse making a solid dissolve more quickly with making more of the solid dissolve. It is important to emphasise that this activity is about making a fixed quantity of a solid dissolve more quickly.

Tell learners to read the instructions in the Learner's Book.

This is a learner-led investigation in which learners compare the time taken for the same quantity of sugar to dissolve in cold and warm water.

> **Practical guidance:** Learners should work in groups of 4–5. Tell learners to allocate a task to each group

member. This will help them think about the different steps they need to follow and ensure that all group members are involved. Tasks can include collecting the equipment and materials, measuring the sugar and water, timing how long it takes the sugar to dissolve, recording the results and putting away the equipment and materials at the end of the activity.

The hot water used should be 'hand hot' only, such as water from a hot tap, and not boiling water from a kettle. The tap water temperature should be about 50 °C, but not hotter.

Check which learners answered 'no' to any of the suggested self-assessment questions below and follow up with them on areas in which they need more support.

> **Assessment ideas:** Learners can answer these self-assessment questions:

Could I:

- make a prediction with reason about whether sugar dissolves more quickly in hot or cold water?
- use my results to say if the prediction was accurate?
- decide if a test is fair?
- make a conclusion from my results and measurements?

3 Demonstrate the effect of temperature on dissolving time (40–50 minutes}

Learning intentions: To demonstrate the effect of temperature on dissolving time.

To observe a pattern in results.

Resources: Five heatproof beakers, laboratory thermometer, water, burner, sugar or coloured crystals such as copper sulfate, teaspoon, measuring cylinder, timer, Worksheet 2.3 (optional)

Description: This is an extension of 'Main teaching idea 2'. The activity can be done as a partial teacher demonstration in which learners help to measure and record the dissolving times of sugar at different temperatures. Learners should make a table to record the temperature measured as well as the time it takes for the sugar to dissolve at that temperature.

They can draw a line graph of the results.

If learners are not able to take part in investigation, they could complete Worksheet 2.3 instead.

> **Practical guidance:** Heat up 100 ml of water for

two minutes. Take the beaker off the burner. Ask a learner to measure the water temperature. Learners should record the temperature in their tables.

Add a teaspoon of sugar or coloured crystals to the beaker. Get another learner to time how long it takes for the sugar or crystals to dissolve.

Heat up 100 ml of water in another beaker for four minutes. Repeat the steps described above to measure and record the water temperature and time taken for the sugar or crystals to dissolve.

Repeat the process with the three other beakers by heating 100 ml of water for 6, 8 and 10 minutes respectively.

Make sure all learners are able to see the demonstration.

Answers

1   Measurements of dissolving time will depend on the water temperature. Learners should observe a pattern in the results which shows that the sugar or crystals dissolve faster as the water temperature increases. Discuss any points on the graph that do not fit the pattern. Ask learners to suggest reasons for this, for example the dissolving time or water temperature were not correctly measured.
2   Graph shapes should look similar to the example below.

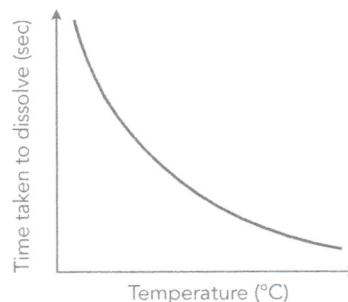

> **Differentiation ideas:** Let learners who need practice in using a thermometer to measure temperature or using a timer do the measuring in the activity.

> **Assessment ideas:** Learners can work in pairs to answer these questions:

Which is the dependent variable in the investigation? (Dissolving time.)

Which is the independent variable in the investigation? (Water temperature.)

Which variables were controlled? (Quantity of water and sugar.)

Use your graph to write a conclusion for the investigation.

They can swap their work with another pair who can assess the answers and graphs using this rubric:

Success criteria	★	★★	★★★
Can correctly identify dependent, independent and control variables.	identifies one or no variables correctly	identifies two or three variables correctly	identifies all variables correctly
Can use the graph to write a conclusion.	writes incorrect conclusion or does not match results in the graph	writes correct conclusion but does not fully explain how the results are linked to the conclusion	writes correct conclusion and explains fully how the results are linked to the conclusion
Can draw a line graph of results.	Does not record temperatures on the x-axis and time on the y-axis; makes more than one error in plotting the data.	Records temperatures on the x-axis and time on the y-axis; makes one error in plotting the data.	Records temperatures and time on the correct axes; makes no errors in plotting the data.

Plenary ideas

1 Talk about it (10–15 minutes)

Resources: A piece of work the learners have completed in the topic

Description: Learners should choose a piece of work they have completed in the topic. They can work in pairs to talk about what they did well in the piece of work and how they think they can improve on it.

> **Assessment ideas:** Learners can give each other feedback on their work using the 'two stars and a wish' strategy.

> **Reflection ideas:** Learners can answer the Reflection questions in the Learner's Book.

2 How well am I doing? (5 minutes)

Resources: Self-assessment questions, such as:

- Can I identify and describe reversible changes?
- Can I say why dissolving is a reversible change?
- Can I say how temperature affects solids dissolving in liquids?
- Can I use the particle model to explain how temperature affects solids dissolving in liquids?

Description: Create and hand out a copy of the questions to each learner or write or project the questions on the board for learners to answer.

> **Assessment ideas:** Ask learners to draw a smiley face if they are happy with their progress and a sad face if they think they need more help.

CROSS-CURRICULAR LINKS

Recording data in a table and drawing a graph in Main teaching idea 3 links with data handling and graphing in Maths.

Writing answers to questions throughout the topic can be linked with sentence construction and vocabulary development in English.

Homework ideas

1 Learners could complete the Activity from the Learner's Book. Discuss answers in class and allow learners to check their own work and make any corrections needed.

2 Learners could complete the Focus, Practice or Challenge Exercises in the Workbook, depending on their progress.

In the next lesson, discuss answers. Learners can work in pairs to check one another's answers.

Topic Worksheet

Worksheet 2.3: Reversible changes

In this worksheet, learners interpret a line graph and identify variables in a fair test. There is a Help sheet to support less confident learners in answering questions 1 and 2. More confident learners can attempt the Stretch questions which involve identifying a pattern in the data, calculating averages, drawing a line graph and explaining results.

2.4 Chemical reactions

LEARNING PLAN

Learning objectives	Learning intentions	Success criteria
6Cc.04 Understand that chemical reactions involve substances, called reactants, interacting to form new substances, called products.	• To find out that in a chemical reaction, substances react together to form new substances. • To identify reactants and products in chemical reactions.	• Learners can understand that in a chemical reaction, substances react together to form new substances. • Learners can identify reactants and products in chemical reactions.
6Cc.05 Observe and describe the evidence that a chemical reaction has taken place (limited to a gas being produced, colour change and change in temperature).	• To observe and describe evidence for chemical reactions.	• Learners can observe and describe evidence for chemical reactions.
6TWSc.08 Collect and record observations and/or measurements in tables and diagrams appropriate to the type of scientific enquiry.	• To make drawings of observations.	• Learners can make drawings of observations.
6TWSc.05 Take appropriately accurate measurements.	• To measure temperature.	• Learners can measure temperature.
6TWSa.03 Make a conclusion from results informed by scientific understanding.	• To use observations to make a conclusion.	• Learners can use observations to make a conclusion.

LANGUAGE SUPPORT

The key terms for this topic are:

react: to interact and change to make a new substance; also to respond to something, for example, the girl reacted to the good news by clapping her hands

reactants: the substances that react together in a chemical reaction

products: the new substances that form in a chemical reaction

evidence: the things we know that show us that something has happened or changed. For example, the footprints in the sand were evidence that someone had walked there

You can help learners become familiar with the new words by getting them to complete sentences using the words. For example:

When we mix vinegar and baking soda, they [react] to make a gas.

Substances like vinegar and baking soda that react together are called [reactants].

New substances, such as gases, that form in a chemical reaction are called [products].

When we see a new gas form, we have [evidence] that a chemical reaction has happened.

Common misconceptions

Misconception	How to identify	How to overcome
Chemical reactions happen when you mix two substances, especially if the colour changes.	Mix together red food dye with a liquid of another colour, e.g. yellow cool drink. Ask learners if a new substance has formed.	Point out that there is colour change because liquids of two different colours were mixed. The substances have not changed. Then do suggested Main activity 1.

Starter ideas

1 Getting started (10–15 minutes)

Resources: Learner's Book, a candle, candle holder, matches, metal teaspoon

Description: This activity recaps on change of state and reversible and irreversible changes.

It is a teacher demonstration. Read the instructions in the Learner's Book before you start.

Learners should work in pairs or small groups to discuss their observations.

Hold a short report-back session for learners to share their answers with the class.

2 Identify chemical reactions (5–10 minutes)

Resources: Digital Classroom: Video: Chemical reactions (optional) or images from the internet of slicing an onion, vinegar and baking soda reaction, burnt toast, dissolving copper sulfate in water, firework sparklers

Description: Ask learners what a chemical reaction is. They should recall this from Stage 4. Ask them to describe any chemical reactions they know of.

> **Digital Classroom:** If you have access to the Digital Classroom component, show the video 'Chemical reactions'. The i button will explain how to use the video.

Alternatively, show the images you found on the internet.

Ask learners which slides show a chemical reaction (vinegar and baking soda reaction, burnt toast, firework sparklers) and why. The answers will tell you if they understand that in a chemical reaction one or more new substances form.

Main teaching ideas

1 Think like a scientist 2: Investigate evidence for chemical reactions A (15–20 minutes)

Learning intentions: To observe and describe evidence for chemical reactions.

To make drawings of observations.

Resources: Learner's Book

Water, cornstarch, iodine solution, a dropper, a spoon, limewater, a drinking straw, beakers

Description: This activity demonstrates that a colour change is an example of evidence for a chemical reaction. This is an example of observing changes over time type of scientific enquiry. Learners should observe that the changes happen quickly.

Learners should read the instructions in the Learner's Book.

At the end of the activity, explain that when starch reacts with iodine, iodine particles combine with particles in the starch to form a new substance.

Limewater (calcium hydroxide) reacts with carbon dioxide in exhaled air to form a new substance (calcium carbonate) which has a milky white colour.

The change in colour is evidence that a new substance has formed.

> **Practical guidance:** This is a learner led activity. Learners should work in groups of 4–5.

Learners should rotate roles in the group, for example, different learners should be allowed to blow air into the limewater and add the iodine solution to the starch.

Learners should not taste any of the chemicals used. Iodine will stain skin and clothes, so tell learners to be careful not to spill the solution.

2 Observe a chemical reaction (10–20 minutes)

Learning intentions: To observe and describe evidence for chemical reactions.

To identify reactants and products in chemical reactions.

Resources: Plaster of Paris, cold water, a wooden spatula such as an ice lolly stick, a disposable cup or small yoghurt cup, measuring spoons, cups or cylinders; Worksheet 2.4 (optional)

Description: In this activity you will demonstrate that a chemical reaction takes place when you mix plaster of Paris with water. A new substance called gypsum forms and heat is given off.

You can ask learners to answer these questions:

1   How do you know that a chemical reaction has taken place?

2   What word do we use for this?

3   Which substances are the reactants?

4   Which substance is the product?

5   Which type of scientific enquiry was used in the demonstration?

Learners can complete the activity by attempting Worksheet 2.4, which uses the plaster of Paris experiment to recap on variables in fair tests.

> **Practical guidance:** The traditional plaster of Paris mix uses two parts of plaster to one part of water. About 100 ml of plaster of Paris and 50 ml water should be enough.

Measure the volume of water first and pour it into the disposable cup. Always add the plaster to the water. Do not add water to dry plaster powder. When you have finished measuring the water, dry the measuring cup thoroughly, or use a separate cup to measure the plaster.

The plaster of Paris reacts with the water and the mixture gets warm as heat is given off. The plaster of Paris takes 10–12 minutes to react and become warm. Small quantities of the reactants such as you are using do not release a lot of heat. It is safe to let learners touch the outside of the cup to feel the heat given off.

Once the plaster is mixed it cannot be changed back into its original form. It will set in the cup. You will have to cut open the cup to remove the set plaster.

Do not put any plaster of Paris down the drain. It will set and cause a blockage.

Answers

1   A new substance forms, heat is given off

2   Evidence

3   Plaster of Paris, water

4   Gypsum

5   Observing over time

> **Differentiation ideas:** Ask more confident learners to do some research to find out how plaster of Paris got its name.

> **Assessment ideas:** Learners can answer these self-assessment questions:

Could I

- say how I know that a chemical reaction took place?

- identify the reactants in the chemical reaction?

- identify the product in the chemical reaction?

3 Think like a scientist 2: Investigate evidence for chemical reactions B (25–30 minutes)

Learning intentions: To observe and describe evidence for chemical reactions.

To measure temperature.

To use observations to make a conclusion.

Resources: Learner's Book

Per group: wire wool, vinegar, beaker, thermometer, timer

Description: In this activity, learners will investigate a change in temperature as evidence for a chemical reaction. The reaction learners will observe in this investigation releases heat as a result of the reaction. In other reactions, heat energy is used and there is a drop in temperature. Read through the instructions in the Learner's Book to make sure learners know what to do.

> **Practical guidance:** This is a learner led activity. Learners should work in groups of 4–5.

In the reaction of vinegar with the wire wool, the vinegar removes the protective coating from the wire wool and speeds up rusting. In the rusting reaction, the iron in the wire wool combines with oxygen in the air and releases heat. This takes about 15 minutes.

> **Differentiation ideas:** More confident learners can extend the investigation by finding out if the quantity of vinegar used in the reaction with the wire wool affects the change in temperature, e.g. does the temperature increase faster, or does it increase more and get hotter?

> **Assessment ideas:** You can use the checklist to assess how well learners worked in the investigation.

Could learners...	yes	partly	needed help
use the materials and equipment correctly?			
measure temperature accurately			
identify evidence for a chemical reaction?			
use observations to write a conclusion?			

Plenary ideas

1 Test tubes (15–20 minutes)

Resources: Per pair: a sheet of paper with outlines of three test tubes containing a liquid (like that below), pens, coloured pencils, sticky putty

Description: Tell learners to work in pairs. Give each pair a sheet with the test tube outlines. Tell them to colour-in the substance in each test tube. On each test tube they should write one thing they have learnt about chemical reactions.

Learners should display their test tubes around the classroom.

They should look at other pairs' test tubes and draw new test tubes for themselves for any other things about chemical reactions they learnt from other learners' answers.

> **Assessment ideas:** Learners can answer these self-assessment questions:

* Do I know at least one thing about chemical reactions?

* What did I learn about chemical reactions from other people's answers?

* Is there anything I do not understand about chemical reactions? If so, what is it?

* > **Reflection ideas:** Learners can answer the Reflection questions from the Learner's Book.

2 Answer questions about chemical reactions (15–20 minutes)

Resources: Learner's Book

Description: Learners can work individually to answer the questions from the Learner's Book about chemical reactions.

> **Assessment ideas:** Choose a different learner to give the answer to each of the questions. Discuss any correct answers and help learners to understand why an answer is wrong.

> **Reflection ideas:** Learners should ask themselves:

What things did I find easy to learn?

What did I find difficult?

How did I deal with the difficult things?

What would I like to know more about?

CROSS-CURRICULAR LINKS

Writing answers to questions throughout the topic can be linked with sentence construction and vocabulary development in English.

Homework ideas

1   Learners could speak to someone at home or in their community who bakes bread to find out why the bread dough rises. (Yeast changes sugars in the bread dough and makes carbon dioxide gas as a product. The bubbles of gas in the dough make it rise). They could also research the information if necessary. Discuss their findings in the next lesson. Ask: What form of evidence is bread dough rising for a chemical reaction? (formation of a gas).

2   Learners could investigate evidence for chemical reactions at home as described below and report back on their findings to the class in the next lesson.

   •   Pour an equal quantity of cold tea into each of the three glasses.

   •   Add a few drops of lemon juice or vinegar to one glass of tea and observe what happens. (The tea becomes paler in colour.)

   •   Add several drops of the liquid dish detergent to another glass of tea and observe what happens. (The tea becomes darker in colour.)

   •   Compare the three glasses of tea. What do you notice? Make a drawing or take photo of your observations.

   •   Name the dependent, independent and control variables in your test. (Dependent variable: colour of the tea; independent variable: substance added to the tea; control variables: quantity of tea, type of tea.)

   •   Did any chemical reactions take place? How do you know. (Yes, chemical reactions take place when we add lemon juice and liquid dish detergent to cold tea because there is a colour change.)

Topic Worksheet

Worksheet 2.4: Chemical reactions

The worksheet for the topic recaps on variables in fair test investigations and evidence for chemical reactions. Learners will also look for a pattern in the data given. There is a Help sheet for learners who may need more support, and more confident learners can be challenged to answer the Stretch questions.

PROJECT: ELECTRICAL INSULATORS

6SIC.04 Identify people who use science, including professionally, in their area and describe how they use science.

6SIC.02 Describe how science is used in their local area.

6TWSc.07 Use a range of secondary information sources to research and select relevant evidence to answer questions.

Learners should work in pairs. They will need to speak to an electrician in their local area to find out how they use electrical insulators in their work.

Learners should then work on their own to find examples of the use of electrical insulators in their homes and local area.

They will also need to do some research from the internet or books to find out about other uses of electrical insulators.

Pairs should then use their individual and combined findings to prepare their presentations. They could make a poster, slideshow or video to present their work.

Assessment rubric

You can use the checklist provided here for peer assessment of the presentations.

How well did [learners' names]	Very well 🙂	Quite well 😐	Not well 🙁
provide information on how an electrician uses electrical insulators?			
provide information on how people use electrical insulators at home and in the local area?			
provide information on other uses of electrical insulators?			
use pictures to show information about electrical conductors?			
present the information in an attractive and interesting way?			

> 3 Rocks, the rock cycle and soil

Unit plan

Topic	Approx. number of learning hours	Outline of learning content	Resources
3.1 Igneous rocks	2	• Learners begin to sort the class rock collection into similar groups and use a key. • They use photographs and diagrams to find out how igneous rocks form and what they consist of. They grow their own crystals.	**Learner's Book:** Think like a scientist 1: Collect and sort rocks Activity: Describe igneous rocks and complete a key Think like a scientist 2: Make your own crystals **Workbook:** Topic 3.1 **Digital Classroom:** Activity – Igneous rocks
3.2 Sedimentary rocks and fossils	2	• Learners continue to sort the class rock collection into similar groups and use a key. • They use photographs and diagrams to find out how sedimentary rocks and fossils form. • They made a model of a plant fossil.	**Learner's Book:** Activity 1: Use text, a photograph and a diagram to describe how sedimentary rocks form Activity 2: Identify and describe sedimentary rocks Think like a scientist: Make your own plant fossil **Workbook:** Topic 3.2 ⬇ Worksheets 3.2 **Digital Classroom:** Video – Sedimentary rocks
3.3 Metamorphic rocks and the rock cycle	2	• Learners continue to sort the class rock collection into similar groups and use a key. • They use photographs and diagrams to find out how metamorphic rocks form. • They use a simple diagram of the rock cycle to see how all three types of rock are continuously changing over time.	**Learner's Book:** Activity 1: Identify and describe metamorphic rocks Think like a scientist: How people use rocks in my area Activity 2: Describe how a model can help us to understand the rock cycle **Workbook:** Topic 3.3 **Digital Classroom:** Video – A mini tour of the Taj Mahal

Topic	Approx. number of learning hours	Outline of learning content	Resources
3.4 Soil	2	• Group activity to investigate a sample of soil. Learners find out about the characteristics of three main types of soil. They find out that the composition of soil can change making it better or worse for plants to grow in it.	**Learner's Book:** Think like a scientist: Investigate a soil sample Activity 1: Types of soil Activity 2: Changing the composition of soil **Workbook:** Topic 3.4 Worksheets 3.4A, 3.4B and 3.4C **Digital Classroom:** Video – Compost

Across unit resources

Learner's Book:

Project: How people use soil

Check your progress quiz

Teacher's Resource:

Language worksheets 1 & 2

Diagnostic test

Mid-year test

End-of-year test

End-of-unit test

Digital Classroom:

End-of-unit quiz

BACKGROUND KNOWLEDGE

In this Unit you introduce your learners to the branch of science called Geology – which means the study of the Earth. You will talk about the three main types of rock and how they form.

Learners are always fascinated by fossils. Fossils give us information about animals and plants that lived on Earth hundreds of millions of years ago.

The lengths of time you refer to are very difficult to imagine. Geological time is measured in millions of years.

Learners may ask you how geologists know how old rocks and fossils are. Geologists can tell how old a rock is by measuring the quantity of certain radioactive elements in the rock. So we can say that the Earth is 4.5 billion years old. Life on Earth dates from about 3.5 billion years ago. Humans only arrived less than 100 000 years ago.

Here is a simple geological timeline which you can use to give examples of when different plants and animals arrived on Earth. We know this because of fossils in the rocks which scientists can measure the age of.

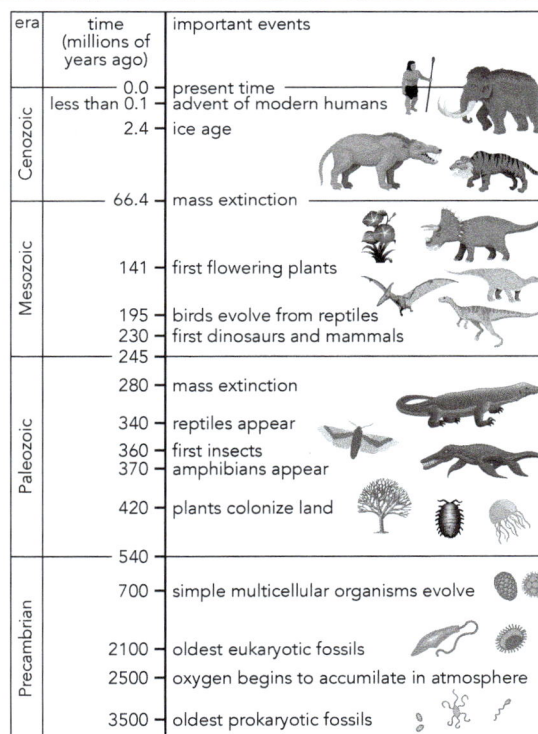

era	time (millions of years ago)	important events
Cenozoic	0.0	present time
	less than 0.1	advent of modern humans
	2.4	ice age
	66.4	mass extinction
Mesozoic	141	first flowering plants
	195	birds evolve from reptiles
	230	first dinosaurs and mammals
	245	
Paleozoic	280	mass extinction
	340	reptiles appear
	360	first insects
	370	amphibians appear
	420	plants colonize land
	540	
Precambrian	700	simple multicellular organisms evolve
	2100	oldest eukaryotic fossils
	2500	oxygen begins to accumulate in atmosphere
	3500	oldest prokaryotic fossils

CONTINUED

For example, from the timeline you can see that:

- the earliest forms of life were in the sea
- the first plants on land arrived 420 million years ago
- the first insects arrived 360 million years ago
- the first dinosaurs and mammals arrived 230 million years ago
- the first flowering plants appeared 141 million years ago.

Learners are always fascinated by dinosaurs and will want to know how they became extinct. You can see on the timeline that there is a mass extinction marked at 66.4 million years ago. Scientists think that this was caused by a massive comet or asteroid 10 to 15 km wide, which crashed into Earth and killed everything on it.

In Topic 3.3 you describe the rock cycle. This is a complicated cycle, but at this stage you only want learners to understand that rock formation is a dynamic process and that rocks are continuously changing – but over millions of years.

In a later stage, learners find out about plate tectonics and discover that the countries as we know them today were joined together and on different parts of the Earth.

In Topic 3.4 you talk about soil. Although soil forms fairly quickly compared to rocks, it still takes several hundred years to make 1 cm³ of soil. All the more reason for us to look after soil.

TEACHING SKILLS FOCUS

Use your surroundings

This Unit is about rocks. Learners will have the opportunity to learn a few basics about geology. It will make a great difference if you can relate the material in this unit to your own country and home region.

You can use the internet to find out the basic geology of your country. For example, the peninsula of India is a huge volcanic plateau made of basalt. In the north of India there are different sedimentary rocks and in the south-east there are metamorphic rocks. Middle Eastern countries consist mainly of sedimentary rocks, especially shale. The Himalayas consist of layers of shale and limestone with igneous intrusions.

Collect some rocks before you start the unit. Collect pictures of rocks. Encourage learners to bring some rock samples to school. In this way you can start a class rock collection. As the topics progress you can keep returning to the class rock collection to find out more about your rocks.

Find out what fossils are found in your country. Talk about these when you teach the topic on fossils. If there's a museum nearby, there may be examples of rocks, fossils or minerals. This would be a great place to visit.

If you live in a city there are plenty of examples of how rocks are used. Outside cities and towns there are quarries where rocks are cut out and used. Here are some examples of how you can see rocks in use:

- Curbstones are often made of igneous or metamorphic rocks which are extremely hard.
- Roads are built from crushed igneous and metamorphic rocks.
- Concrete is made from limestone.
- Roofs and floors are sometimes made from slate.
- Bricks are made from clay.
- Glass is made from sand.
- Marble is used for floors and tables and statues.
- Company headquarters and big banks often have polished granite and marble walls in their entrance halls.

When you teach the topic on igneous rocks you will talk about minerals and crystals – semi-precious and precious stones such as diamonds, emeralds and rubies are all examples of minerals.

3.1 Igneous rocks

LEARNING PLAN

Learning objectives	Learning intention	Success criteria
6ESp.01 Know rocks can be classified as metamorphic, igneous and sedimentary and describe the identifying features of each type of rock.	• Find out that rocks can be classified into different types and describe the features of each.	• Learners can find out that rocks can be classified into different types and describe the features of each.
6ESc.01 Describe the rock cycle, and the formation of metamorphic, igneous and sedimentary rocks, in terms of magma and solidification.	• Describe the formation of igneous rocks, in terms of magma and solidification.	• Learners can describe the formation of igneous rocks.
6TWSm.02 Use models, including diagrams, to represent and describe scientific phenomena and ideas.	• Use diagrams and photographs to describe igneous rocks.	• Learners can use diagrams and photographs to describe igneous rocks.
6TWSp.03 Make predictions, referring to relevant scientific knowledge and understanding within familiar and unfamiliar contexts.	• Make predictions, based on what we know about how igneous rocks form.	• Learners can make predictions, based on what we know about how igneous rocks form.
6TWSp.05 Describe risks when planning practical work and consider how to minimise them.	• Describe risks when planning practical work and carry out practical work safely.	• Learners can describe risks when planning practical work and carry out practical work safely.
6TWSc.06 Carry out practical work safely.	• Describe risks when planning practical work and carry out practical work safely.	• Learners can describe risks when planning practical work and carry out practical work safely.
6TWSc.01 Sort, group and classify objects, materials and living things through testing, observation and using secondary information.	• Sort and group rocks by observing differences.	• Learners can sort and group rocks by observing differences.
6TWSc.02 Complete a key based on easily observed differences.	• Complete a key to igneous rocks based on easily observed differences.	• Learners can complete a key to igneous rocks based on easily observed differences.
6TWSa.01 Describe the accuracy of predictions, based on results.	• Describe the accuracy of predictions, based on results.	• Learners can describe the accuracy of predictions, based on results.

LANGUAGE SUPPORT

Learners will use the following words:

geologist: a scientist who studies rocks

igneous rock: a rock which comes from magma that has cooled down into solid rock. In English the verb 'to ignite' means to set fire to something. You start up an engine by turning the key for the ignition

solidification: the process where liquid magma or lava cools down and becomes solid rock

extrusive igneous rock: (ex-troo-siv) an igneous rock that has formed from lava cooling down on the surface of the Earth. 'Ex' always refers to something outside, e.g. exit means the way outside

intrusive igneous rock: (in-troo-siv) an igneous rock that has formed when magma cools down inside the Earth's crust. 'Intrusive' means something that

forces its way inside. In this context the magma is forcing its way into the Earth's crust

mineral: part of a rock made of different substances with a crystalline structure. Examples: quartz, feldspar

crystal: (cri-stal) the particular shaped structure of a mineral

crystalline: The adjective for crystal. So we describe an igneous rock as crystalline because it is made up of crystals

naked eye: this expression means we can see something with our eyes without the help of a magnifying glass or hand lens

sedimentary rock: a rock made from small pieces of other rock stuck together

Starter ideas

1 Getting started (10–15 minutes)

Resources: Learner's Book

Description: These questions revise what learners did about the internal structure of the Earth in Stage 4. This is important background for this unit. Let learners answer questions in pairs and then share with the class.

2 Lava flows (5 minutes)

Resources: Learner's Book – topic opening photographs

Description: *Ask learners: What is shown on the photograph?* (A volcano, lava, lava flow.)

Where has the lava come from?
(From magma in the Earth's crust.)

Why is some of the lava red and some black?
(The red lava is still flowing and the black lava is cooling down and forming rock.)

Main teaching ideas

1 Think like a scientist 1: Collect and sort rocks (30 minutes)

Learning intentions: Sort and group rocks by observing differences

Resources: Learner's Book, a selection of different rocks, some hand lenses, if possible one per group

Description: Divide the class into groups of about ten learners. Give each group a selection of different rocks.

Tell learners to answer questions 1–3 in their group.

Discuss their findings so far in class.

Hopefully you will have some sedimentary and some igneous or metamorphic rocks in your collection which will make it possible for learners to sort their rocks into two groups (question 4 – the learning intention).

These are sedimentary rocks, which are one main colour and consist of grains stuck together, and igneous rocks, which have shiny crystals and may have several colours and a spotted appearance. (These could also be metamorphic rocks but we will be looking at that possibility later in the topic.)

Pack each group's rocks in a bag and keep for later in the topic.

> **Practical guidance:** Tell learners a week or two before the lesson to collect rocks and bring them to school. Warn them not to collect 'manufactured' materials like concrete and brick. Places they can look are rock cuttings where a road passes through and the rocks are exposed or a quarry where rock is being cut out to use for building materials, or a building site. Tell them to ask an older sibling or parent to help them collect rocks.

Safety: they should be careful not to fall or climb any steep rock faces!

They must put a label on each rock with their name and the place where they found the rock and bring their rock samples to class.

You should also collect as many different rocks as you can.

If you only manage to find a few rocks you will have to do this activity as a teacher demonstration. Pass the rocks round so that all the learners can look at them and feel them.

> **Assessment ideas:** As you walk around the class you can observe how learners are working in their groups.

Are there dominant learners who take control?

Are there learners who don't contribute at all?

2 Activity: Describe igneous rocks and complete a key (60 minutes)

Learning intentions: Find out that rocks can be classified into different types and describe the features of each.

Explain the formation of igneous rocks, in terms of magma and solidification.

Use diagrams and photographs to describe igneous rocks.

Sort and group rocks by observing differences.

Complete a key to igneous rocks based on easily observed differences.

Resources: Learner's Book

Samples of igneous rocks and/or photographs of igneous rocks from books

Samples of crystals and/or photographs of crystals from books

Description: There are quite a lot of new words in this section – refer to the 'Language support' section.

Begin by telling the learners that the word 'igneous' comes from a Greek word meaning 'fire'. So igneous rocks are formed from fire-like magma and lava.

Next you explain how igneous rocks form. Focus on the diagram to use as a model to show how igneous rocks are formed. This is a three dimensional representation that shows what is happening below the Earth's surface and what is on the Earth's surface.

Describe how extrusive igneous rocks form using the diagram and the photographs on the opening pages of the topic. The most common extrusive

igneous rock is basalt which is a black rock. If you have a sample of basalt, show the class.

Next explain how intrusive igneous rocks form – use the diagram. Show learners the mass of granite inside the Earth's crust. We can only see the granite at the surface of the Earth when the layers of rock above it wear away (which takes millions of years! – see Background knowledge notes).

If you have a sample of igneous rock like granite to show learners they can see it contains different things. You can see this clearly in the photograph of granite in the Learner's Book. Now move on to explain what the 'different things' are under 'What are igneous rocks made of?'

If you have some crystals or photographs of crystals, show learners at this point.

Use the photograph of granite in the Learner's Book to show the crystals of different minerals in granite. Point out that we can see the different crystals with our eyes – we don't need a magnifying glass. This is called seeing with 'the naked eye'. The crystals are large because the magma cooled slowly inside the Earth's crust.

Show learners the photograph of basalt – this contains the same minerals as granite but we can't see the individual crystals because they are too small. They are very small because the lava cooled quickly on the surface of the Earth.

Learners can consolidate what they have learnt in this section by answering the questions in Activity: Describe igneous rocks and complete a key. They can work on their own or in pairs and write their answers in their notebooks.

> **Differentiation ideas:** Some learners may struggle with the vocabulary or with understanding the diagram. Take time and explain everything more than once. Get learners to work in pairs so that they can help each other.

> **Assessment ideas:** Go through answers to the questions in class before moving on to the next section.

3 Think like a scientist 2: Make your own crystals (40 minutes + a week for crystals to grow)

Learning intentions: Describe risks when planning practical work and carry out practical work safely.

Make predictions, based on what we know about how igneous rocks form.

Describe the accuracy of predictions, based on results.

Make a conclusion from results using scientific understanding.

Resources: Learner's Book

Two glass jars, two paper clips, two pencils, two 10 cm pieces of string, a cup of coarse salt, hot water, a teaspoon

Description: Do this as a teacher demonstration.

Encourage learners to do the same activity at home and bring their crystals to school. They could use potassium permanganate or copper sulphate for different coloured crystals. These are available at pharmacies. Salt crystals are more easily available and cheap to buy.

Explain the purpose of the activity before you begin. We are going to grow crystals in a cold environment (modelling lava cooling on the surface of the Earth) and a warm environment (modelling magma cooling inside the Earth). We will compare how quickly the crystals grow in the two environments and we will compare the sizes of the crystals that grow in the two environments.

Learners can answer questions 1–3 in their notebooks. They can leave space for answers to questions 4–7 and answer these later when the crystals have formed.

> **Practical guidance:** Before you begin, tell learners that they will have to handle hot water during the activity. Ask them to say how you can minimise the risk of burning yourself.

Follow the instructions in the Learner's Book.

The more saturated with salt you make your solution the quicker the crystals will grow. When you have stirred and dissolved as much salt into the hot water as you can, you could heat the solution up again and add more salt crystals.

Make two learners responsible for checking each jar every day. They must unwind the string so that the paper clip is always in the salt solution. They must report back to class as soon as they see crystals forming on the paper clip.

> **Differentiation ideas:** The activity is simple to do but some learners may find it difficult to see jars 1 and 2 as models of crystals forming in intrusive and extrusive igneous rock. Make sure you explain this carefully. Go back to the diagram of intrusive and extrusive igneous rocks to point out the two

environments – cooler on the surface in the air and hotter inside the Earth near the magma.

> **Assessment ideas:** Go through answers in class in stages: 1–3 when you have set up the jars and 4–7 a week later when the crystals have formed.

4 Analyse a sample of igneous rock (20 minutes)

Learning intentions: Find out that rocks can be classified into different types and describe the features of each.

Explain the formation of igneous rocks in terms of magma and solidification.

Resources: A sample of igneous rock

Description: This activity does not appear in the Learner's Book.

Learners can answer these questions about their sample:

1   How do you know this is an igneous rock?

2   What minerals can you identify in the rock?

3   Was this rock formed when magma cooled inside the Earth's crust or was it formed when lava cooled at the surface? Give reasons.

4   Suggest what type of igneous rock this is.

> **Practical guidance:** Hand out samples of igneous rock. Learners can work in pairs or groups according to how many samples you have.

They can swap rock samples and answer the questions for a different sample.

Answers

1   Learners should look for characteristics such as being crystalline and having a mottled appearance.

2   In rocks such as granite they will be able to identify quartz, feldspar and mica (see labelled sample of granite in the Learner's Book).

3   If the rock shows all the different crystals, the magma must have cooled down slowly and large crystals formed. If you can't see the crystals the lava cooled quickly on the surface.

4   If crystals are large, it could be granite. If you can't see crystals and the rock is black, it could be basalt.

> **Differentiation ideas:** As you walk around the class, find out which learners are having trouble with some of the questions. Advise them if necessary. Refer them back to the relevant information in the Learner's Book.

> **Assessment ideas:** Learners can compare their answers about each sample in a class feedback session.

Plenary ideas

1 Know your igneous rock words (10 minutes)

Resources: 3–5 cards for each of these words (so, 21–35 cards in total): extrusive igneous rock, intrusive igneous rock, crystalline, magma, solidification, mineral, fire. Digital Classroom activity: Igneous rocks (optional)

Description: Divide the class into pairs. Give each pair a card. Ask the following questions. (The pairs with the correct answer on their card must hold up their card.)

What is an igneous rock that forms on the surface of the Earth?
(Extrusive igneous rock)

What do igneous rocks form from?
(Magma)

What does the word 'igneous' mean?
(Fire)

What type of igneous rock forms inside the Earth's crust?
(Intrusive igneous rock)

What process causes magma to form igneous rock?
(Solidification)

What is the most important characteristic of igneous rock?
(Crystalline)

What are quartz and feldspar?
(Minerals)

> **Digital Classroom:** If you have access to the Digital Classroom component, use the activity 'Igneous rocks' to consolidate learners knowledge from this topic. The i button will explain how to the use the activity.

> **Assessment ideas:** This game will give you an opportunity to see if there are any learners who do not know the meaning of some of the key words.

> **Reflection ideas:** See the Learner's Book at end of the topic.

2 Workbook: Focus exercise (10 minutes)

Resources: Workbook

Description: A straightforward activity suitable for all learners that will consolidate the main points of the topic.

> **Assessment ideas:** Go through the answers in class.

> **Reflection ideas:** See the Learner's Book at the end of the topic.

CROSS-CURRICULAR LINKS

Plenary idea 1 links to English (new vocabulary).

Homework ideas

1   Workbook: Practice exercise.

    In this exercise learners must label a diagram they have not seen before using their knowledge from the topic.

2   Workbook: Challenge exercise.

    In this exercise learners apply what they have learnt to identify some rocks that Arun and Marcus see on the sea shore.

3   Find out what igneous rocks there are in your country.

    Did the igneous rocks form inside the Earth's crust? Or did they form as a result of lava cooling at the surface?

    Find a picture of these rocks in your country and bring it to class.

3.2 Sedimentary rocks and fossils

LEARNING PLAN

Learning objectives	Learning intention	Success criteria
6ESp.01 Know rocks can be classified as metamorphic, igneous and sedimentary and describe the identifying features of each type of rock.	• Find out that rocks can be classified into different types and describe the features of each.	• Learners can find out that rocks can be classified into different types and describe the features of each.
6ESc.01 Describe the rock cycle, and the formation of metamorphic, igneous and sedimentary rocks, in terms of magma, solidification, erosion, sedimentation, burial, metamorphism and melting.	• Explain the formation of sedimentary rocks, in terms of weathering, erosion and sedimentation.	• Learners can explain the formation of sedimentary rocks, in terms of weathering, erosion and sedimentation.
6ESp.02 Describe the way fossils can form in sedimentary rocks.	• Describe the way fossils can form in sedimentary rocks.	• Learners can describe the way fossils can form in sedimentary rocks.
6TWSm.02 Use models, including diagrams, to represent and describe scientific phenomena and ideas.	• Use diagrams and photographs to describe sedimentary rocks.	• Learners can use diagrams and photographs to describe sedimentary rocks.
6TWSc.01 Sort, group and classify materials through observation.	• Sort and group rocks by observing differences.	• Learners can sort and group rocks by observing differences.
6TWSc.02 Complete a key based on easily observed differences.	• Complete a key to sedimentary rocks based on easily observed differences.	• Learners can complete a key to sedimentary rocks based on easily observed differences.

LANGUAGE SUPPORT

Learners will use the following words:

sediment: very small pieces of rock

sedimentation: the process where sediments build up in layers on the sea bed or on a lake bed

weathering: a process where heat, ice, rain or plant roots break up rocks

erode: to wear down weathered rocks into sediments. The noun is 'erosion'. Erosion can be done by rivers, ice or wind

transport: to carry. The noun is 'transportation'. In this topic we are talking about sediments being transported by a river to the sea. We use the words 'transport' and 'transportation' in everyday English to mean buses, cars, trains, bicycles etc., which transport us from one place to another

valley: the landform that a river erodes in the rocks. A river flows in a valley

> **CONTINUED**
>
> **deposit:** to put down or drop. The noun is deposition
>
> In this topic we are talking about how a river transports sediments and then deposits them on the sea bed or on a lake bed.
>
> **fossil:** the preserved remains of animals and plants in sedimentary rocks
>
> **preserved:** kept for a very long time
>
> **mould:** a fossil which makes an impression in rock of exactly the same shape and size as the animal
>
> or plant container used to pour liquid metal into to make a shape. Or we use a mould in cooking to make desserts such as jellies.
>
> Or the word 'mould' has a completely different meaning – a growth of fungi that you get on fruit or bread that is left in a damp place.
>
> **cast:** a fossil where the bones of the whole animal are preserved in minerals. In everyday English the verb 'to cast' has several meanings, for example: to cast your vote in an election; to cast your fishing line into the water.

Starter ideas

1 Getting started (10–15 minutes)

Resources: Learner's Book

Description: Look at the photograph of the canyon.

Ask learners the questions in the Learner's Book.

This will be a good introduction to the topic because learners will already be able to tell you the most important characteristic of sedimentary rocks – that they form in layers.

2 Igneous and sedimentary rocks (10 minutes)

Resources: A piece of granite (or other crystalline igneous rock) and a piece of sandstone or limestone or shale

Description: Hold up the igneous rock. Ask: *What rock is this?*
(An igneous rock/granite)

What is the main characteristic of this rock?
(It is crystalline)

Hold up the sedimentary rock.

How is this rock different to the igneous rock?
(It is not crystalline, it is one colour, it is grainy.)

Main teaching ideas

1 What are sedimentary rocks? (45 minutes)

Learning intentions: Find out that rocks can be classified into different types and describe the features of each.

Use diagrams and photographs to describe sedimentary rocks.

Explain the formation of sedimentary rocks, in terms of weathering, erosion and sedimentation.

Resources: Learner's Book; Digital Classroom video: Sedimentary rocks (optional)

Description: There are a lot of new words in this section. Use the 'Language support' section to help you to explain the new words and help learners with pronunciation.

Read through the text. It is important that learners understand the stages in the process of how sediments are formed from other, existing rocks and then these sediments are deposited in layers which later become rock. The whole process takes millions of years!

The most important characteristic of sedimentary rocks is that they form in layers – show learners the photograph of the canyon at the beginning of the topic. This photograph shows the layers very well. Tell learners this probably took hundreds of millions of years to form!

The diagram is a section through the Earth, the sea and the sea bed. Get learners to point to the following stages shown on the diagram:

- Material eroded from the land and transported by rivers and ice.
- Sediments deposited in the sea
- Sedimentation
- Over time the bottom layers turn into sedimentary rock.

Learners can consolidate what they have learnt by doing Activity 1: Use text, a photograph and a diagram to describe how sedimentary rocks form. They can work alone or in pairs. Each learner should write answers in their notebook.

> **Digital Classroom:** If you have access to the Digital Classroom component, show the video 'Sedimentary rocks'. The i button will explain how to use the video.

> **Differentiation ideas:** Some learners will take longer to remember the new words and work out the sequences of events than others. Consider working in pairs so that one partner can help the other.

> **Assessment ideas:** Go through answers in class before moving on to the next section.

2 Types of sedimentary rocks (30 minutes)

Learning intentions: Find out that rocks can be classified into different types and describe the features of each.

Use diagrams and photographs to describe sedimentary rocks.

Sort and group rocks by observing differences.

Complete a key to sedimentary rocks based on easily observed differences.

Resources: Learner's Book

Samples of sedimentary rock; Worksheet 3.2 (optional)

Description: Read the text about the three most common types of sedimentary rocks: sandstone, limestone and shale.

Look at the photographs. Point out the layers shown in each photograph.

Learners may ask you how come the layers of rock are now on land when they formed below the sea. This is a difficult question to answer at this stage. In later stages they learn about plate tectonics and Earth movements. But for now you could say that as more and more sediments are deposited, the balance between the land and sea bed changes and there are Earth movements. The sea bed becomes dry land. And all this happens over many millions of years.

To practise sorting sedimentary rocks into sandstone, limestone and shale, learners do Activity 2: Identify and describe sedimentary rocks.

Learners can consolidate their knowledge by completing Worksheet 3.2, which describes a use for sedimentary and igneous rock.

> **Practical guidance:** Divide learners into the same groups they were in at the beginning of the unit. Hand out bags of rocks to each group so that they can answer questions 1–3.

Learners write answers to all the questions in their notebooks.

> **Differentiation ideas:** Some learners may find the key confusing. Consider pairing them with a learner who finds it easy to use and can share their knowledge.

> **Assessment ideas:** Groups can compare answers in class before moving on to the next section.

Get learners to assess their skills at using a key in the 'How am I doing?' question at the end of the activity.

3 Think like a scientist: Make your own plant fossil (45 minutes)

Learning intentions: Describe the way fossils can form in sedimentary rocks.

Resources: Learner's Book

Examples of fossils if possible or photographs of fossils in books or on the internet

Description: Learners find this topic fascinating. They may ask you questions about how old fossils are or why animals (like dinosaurs) became extinct – find the answers to all these questions in Background Knowledge section at the beginning of this Unit.

If you have some real fossils for learners to look at and touch this will be great.

Read the section about fossils and discuss the photographs. For example, ask learners how they think the dinosaur was fossilised (animal died at the edge of a large lake or sea, became covered in sediments which eventually became rock). Tell them about when dinosaurs existed and when they became extinct (see Background knowledge). Point out that plants become fossilised as well as animals and look at the example in the photograph.

Fossil casts are often very beautiful because they are crystalline, as you can see in the ammonite fossil in the photograph.

When you have discussed the different ways in which fossils form, you can demonstrate making your own 'fossil' and/or learners can make their own – see below for practical guidance.

Learners must answer questions 1 and 2, which appear after the practical instructions, in their notebooks.

If you find the class is really interested in fossils you could read about the West Coast Fossil Park which is in the Challenge exercise of the Workbook.

> **Practical guidance:** For the practical activity you will need some plasticine, some plaster of Paris (available from hardware shop or supermarket) and a leaf with veins which stick out so that they make an impression in the plasticine.

You could demonstrate steps 1–3 in class, and show them a finished 'fossil' which you have already made.

Then learners can work in pairs to do this activity. You may find it is easier if they make the fossil at home and bring it to class. Learners don't have to use a leaf to make a fossil, they can use a sea shell or dead beetle, for example.

> **Assessment ideas:** Display learners' fossil casts in the classroom.

Go through answers to questions 1 and 2 in class.

4   Find a fossil (20 minutes)

Learning intentions: Describe the way fossils can form in sedimentary rocks.

Use a range of secondary information sources to research and select relevant evidence to answer questions.

Resources: Library book or internet

Description: Learners should find a picture of a fossil, then answer the following questions about it:

1   Name the fossil
2   How old is the fossil?
3   What type of rock is the fossil in?
4   How did the fossil form?

Present a picture of the fossil and your answers on an A4 page.

Differentiation: Many learners enjoy searching for information. For others this may prove difficult – tell learners to ask for help if they need it.

Answers

Learners will find the answers to questions 1–3 in the reference they use.

For question 4 they can refer back to the Learner's Book to see whether the fossil is a mould or a cast.

> **Assessment ideas:** Display learners' information about fossils in class for everyone to share.

Plenary ideas

1   Know your sedimentary rock words (10 minutes)

Resources: Make a card for each of these words: sedimentary rock, sedimentation, weathering, erosion, valley, transportation, deposition, shale, limestone, fossil, mould, cast

Description: Divide class into pairs. Give each pair a card. Ask the following questions. (The pair with the correct answer on their card must hold up their card.)

Which rocks are made of broken up pieces of other rocks?
(Sedimentary rock)

What is breaking up rocks with heat and cold called?
(Weathering)

What is the hollow the river cuts out of the rocks called?
(Valley)

What word describes how a river uses broken up rocks to cut out a valley?
(Erosion)

What word describes how a river carries sediments?
(Transportation)

What word describes how a river drops sediments in a lake or the sea?
(Deposition)

What is the process called when sediments build up in layers on the sea bed?
(Sedimentation)

Which sedimentary rock is made from broken up shells?
(Limestone)

Which sedimentary rock is made from very fine-grained sediments?
(Shale)

What do we call an animal's remains preserved in rock?
(A fossil)

What type of fossil is an imprint of the animal or plant?
(A mould)

If a mould fills with minerals, what type of fossil do we get?
(A cast)

> **Assessment ideas:** This game will give you an opportunity to see if there are any learners who do not know the meaning of some of the key words. Re-enforce any words that learners are still finding difficult by referring back to where the words are used in the Learner's Book.

2   Igneous or sedimentary (10 minutes)

Resources: A sample of igneous rock and a sample of sedimentary rock and a sample of rock with a fossil in it

Description: Hold up each rock in turn (or photograph of a rock if you have not got a sample).

Ask these questions:

Is this an igneous rock or a sedimentary rock?

How do you know?

The key answer will be that Igneous rocks are crystalline and sedimentary rocks are not crystalline.

If the rock has several colours it is igneous (but remember basalt is igneous and is only black).

The rock with the fossil in has to be a sedimentary rock.

> **Assessment ideas:** If learners are not able to distinguish between the rocks they need some more consolidation and practice they should do the Workbook exercises Focus and Practice.

Homework ideas

1   Workbook: Focus or Practice activities.

They give opportunities for consolidation of the Topic and recognising rocks and fossils from pictures.

2   Workbook: Challenge activity.

This is a short case study about an amazing fossil park in South Africa that should interest learners.

3   Find out what fossils can be found in rocks in your country. Give some examples of the names of the fossils, the rocks they are found in and where in your country they can be found. Bring your information to class.

Topic Worksheet

Worksheet 3.2: Sedimentary rocks and fossils

This Worksheet provides a description of what concrete is made from (sedimentary and igneous rock) and what it is used for. Learners read the information, answer questions and draw a bar graph. The Help sheet provides support to learners who need help to answer the questions and guides them through drawing the bar graph. The Stretch questions are for learners who need more of a challenge.

CROSS-CURRICULAR LINKS
Percentages and bar graphs in the Worksheet can be linked with Mathematics.

3.3 Metamorphic rocks and the rock cycle

LEARNING PLAN		
Learning objectives	**Learning intention**	**Success criteria**
6ESp.01 Know rocks can be classified as metamorphic, igneous and sedimentary and describe the identifying features of each type of rock.	• Describe the features of metamorphic rocks and how they form.	• Learners can describe the features of metamorphic rocks and how they form.
6TWSm.02 Use models, including diagrams, to represent and describe scientific phenomena and ideas.	• Use diagrams and photographs to describe metamorphic rocks.	• Learners can use diagrams and photographs to describe metamorphic rocks.
6ESc.01 Describe the rock cycle, and the formation of metamorphic, igneous and sedimentary rocks, in terms of magma, solidification, erosion, sedimentation, burial, metamorphism and melting.	• Describe the rock cycle, and the formation of metamorphic, igneous and sedimentary rocks, in terms of magma, solidification, erosion, sedimentation, burial, metamorphism and melting.	• Learners can describe the rock cycle, and the formation of metamorphic, igneous and sedimentary rocks, in terms of magma, solidification, erosion, sedimentation, burial, metamorphism and melting.

CONTINUED

Learning objectives	Learning intention	Success criteria
6TWSm.01 Describe how a model can help us understand and describe scientific phenomena and ideas.	• Describe how a model can help us understand the rock cycle.	• Learners can describe how a model can help us understand the rock cycle.
6TWSc.01 Sort, group and classify materials and living things through testing, observation and using secondary information.	• Sort and group rocks by observing differences.	• Learners can sort and group rocks by observing differences.
6TWSc.02 Complete a key based on easily observed differences.	• Complete a key to metamorphic rocks based on easily observed differences.	• Learners can complete a key to metamorphic rocks based on easily observed differences.
6TWSc.07 Use a range of secondary information sources to research and select relevant evidence to answer questions.	• Use reference material to identify rocks used in your community.	• Learners can identify rocks used in your community.

LANGUAGE SUPPORT

Learners will use the following words:

metamorphic rock: a rock that has been changed by heat or pressure or both heat and pressure, for example quartzite, marble and slate

mass: a large intrusion of igneous rock. This can be several thousand cubic kilometres in size. The word 'mass' is used in general to mean a large quantity. For example, a mass of people

burial: burying of sediments with many layers of sediments above. In everyday English 'burial' is the act of laying a person to rest in the ground.

gneiss: metamorphic rock made from granite. This word is pronounced the same as 'nice'

Starter ideas

1 Getting started (5 minutes)

Photograph at start of topic

Description: Tell learners that the whole interior of the building has been carved from rock. Why do you think people chose this rock?

Answers may include:

- it must be very hard
- it has beautiful colours
- it is shiny.

2 Igneous and sedimentary rocks (10 minutes)

Resources: A sample or picture of each type of rock

Description: Ask learners the three questions:

What is the most important characteristic of all igneous rocks? (Crystalline)

What is the most important characteristic of all sedimentary rocks? (It is formed in layers.)

Why don't we find fossils in igneous rocks? (Because igneous rocks are magma and lava that have cooled down.)

This will make sure learners are clear about igneous and sedimentary rock before moving on to the third type of rock, metamorphic. We will be learning about this type of rock in this topic

Main teaching ideas

1 What are metamorphic rocks? (45 minutes)

Learning intention: Describe the features of metamorphic rocks and how they form.

Use diagrams and photographs to describe metamorphic rocks.

Sort and group rocks by observing differences.

Complete a key to metamorphic rocks based on easily observed differences.

Resources: Learner's Book

Some samples of metamorphic rocks.

Photographs of metamorphic rocks and statues and buildings made of metamorphic rocks.

Description: Read through the text under 'What are metamorphic rocks?' and then 'What causes the heat and pressure?'

Look at the diagram of the intrusive igneous mass. Point out that this mass can be thousands of cubic kilometres in size!

Tell learners to point to the rocks on the diagram which will be metamorphosed (the rocks next to the igneous mass).

Move on to 'Types of metamorphic rock'. In this section learners will see how the sedimentary and igneous rocks they learnt about in earlier topics change into metamorphic rocks.

Finish this section with Activity 1: Identify and describe metamorphic rocks. Learners can answer questions 1–4 and question 6 in their notebooks.

> **Practical guidance:** For question 5 learners must work in their group and get their bag of rocks. This time they are looking for rocks which could be metamorphic rocks. They use a key to help them to identify the type of metamorphic rock.

Differentiation: Understanding metamorphic rocks is quite challenging – even the words are difficult! The huge time scale of how rocks form is very difficult to imagine. So some learners will need several explanations before they begin to understand.

> **Assessment ideas:** Go through answers in class before moving on to the rock cycle.

2 Think like a scientist: How people use rocks in my area (10 minutes class time and 60 minutes out of class time)

Learning intention: Describe the features of metamorphic rocks and how they form.

Use reference material to identify rocks used in your community.

Resources: Learner's Book; Digital Classroom video: A mini tour of the Taj Mahal (optional)

Description: Because metamorphic rocks are very hard they are useful for building roads. Rocks such as marble are beautiful when polished so they are often used for carving statues and decorating buildings. More examples are given in the Learner's Book under Think like a scientist 1: How people use rocks in my area.

Have a class discussion where learners think of how metamorphic rocks are used in your local area. They can also say how metamorphic rocks are used for famous buildings and monuments in your country (for example the Taj Mahal in India is built of marble).

This is a good way to demonstrate the Science in Context objective: 6SIC.02 Describe how science is used in their local area.

> **Digital Classroom:** If you have access to the Digital Classroom component, show the video 'A mini tour of the Taj Mahal' to consolidate discussions. The i button will explain how to use the video.

> **Practical guidance:** Give learners a week to do this activity.

They can work in pairs. They may need to find an older sibling or relative to visit places with them and take photographs.

Answers

Share findings with the class

> **Differentiation ideas:** Some learners may surprise you because this sort of activity appeals to them and they enjoy finding information with their family. Other learners may struggle to find examples. Give encouragement to these learners.

> **Assessment ideas:** Praise learners for their efforts. Display photographs in the classroom

3 The rock cycle (45 minutes)

Learning intentions: Describe the rock cycle, and the formation of metamorphic, igneous and sedimentary rocks in terms of magma, solidification, erosion, sedimentation, burial, metamorphism, and melting.

Describe how a model can help us understand the rock cycle.

Resources: Learner's Book

Description: Remind learners of the water cycle, which they learnt about in Stage 5.

The water in the water cycle is used and re-used over and over again.

It is the same principle with the rock cycle. However, the time it takes for rocks to form and re-form is enormous – hundreds of millions of years.

In this section you must focus on the diagram of the rock cycle (which is very simplified). This is a very good exercise in describing how a model can help them to understand the rock cycle. The model is the diagram. It would be impossible to see the whole cycle in real life.

Learners must look at the arrows and follow the cycle with their fingers as suggested in the Learner's Book. The first example begins with magma.

They can practise starting at different points on the cycle and describing what will happen next.

Finish by answering the questions in Activity 2: Describe how a model can help us understand the rock cycle in their notebooks.

> **Differentiation ideas:** Some learners will find this difficult. Spend time talking through different parts of the model until everyone is more confident.

> **Assessment ideas:** Go through answers to questions in class

4 The geological history from granite to sandstone to quartzite (20 minutes)

Learning intention: Describe the features of metamorphic rocks and how they form.

Describe the rock cycle, and the formation of metamorphic, igneous and sedimentary rocks in terms of magma, solidification, erosion, sedimentation, burial, metamorphism and melting.

Resources: Diagram of rock cycle in Learner's Book

Description: This activity does not appear in the Learner's Book.

Show learners the diagram of the rock cycle in the Learner's Book.

Ask learners to use the rock cycle to describe how, over millions of years, granite can become sandstone and then quartzite.

Answers

Granite erodes to form sediments which are deposited on the sea bed. Layers build up and the layers at the bottom become rock. The rock is buried below the Earth's crust. It is close to an igneous mass and heat causes the sandstone to melt and re-crystallise into quartzite.

> **Differentiation ideas:** This is quite a challenging activity.

For learners who don't quite know where to start, you can help them by telling them to copy and complete this passage and then continue the story:

Granite erodes to form _____ which are deposited on the sea _____ . Layers build up and the layers at the bottom become _____ . The rock is buried below the Earth's _____ . It is close to an igneous mass…

> **Assessment ideas:** Discuss the answers in class. The wording does not have to be exactly the same as the story above. Also, learners could draw the story rather than describe it in words.

Plenary ideas

1 Use the rock cycle (10 minutes)

Resources: Diagram of the rock cycle

Description: Ask learners to give examples of each part of the rock cycle. For example:

Give an example of an igneous rock; give an example of weathering, etc..

This will help to bring together everything they have learnt about rocks.

> **Assessment ideas:** Use the 'How am I doing?' self-assessment at the end of this topic.

> **Reflection ideas:** How does the diagram of the rock cycle help you to understand how rocks are re-used and changed over and over again?

2 Describe the rock cycle in sentences (10 minutes)

Resources: Diagram of the rock cycle

Description: Ask learners in turn to describe in sentences what is happening at different points of the rock cycle. This will help them to improve their English speaking skills as well as understand the processes involved in the rock cycle.

Example:

Igneous rock weathers and erodes to form sediments. Sediments build up in layers on the sea bed during the sedimentation process.

> **Assessment ideas:** Use the 'How am I doing?' self-assessment at the end of this topic.

> **Reflection ideas:** How does the diagram of the rock cycle help you to understand how rocks are re-used and changed over and over again?

Homework ideas

1 Workbook: Focus exercise.

This activity gives learners the opportunity to recall key words from the topic.

2 Workbook: Practice or Challenge exercise.

The Practice activity gives learners practice in filling in a key and completing a diagram of the rock cycle. For those learners who are more confident with the rock cycle, the Challenge activity gives them an opportunity to draw their own rock cycle diagram from a description.

3 Find an object such as an ornament, a table or a chopping board at home or in a shop that is made of metamorphic rock. Then:

- Make a drawing of it or take a photograph of it.

- Identify the rock it is made of.

- Describe why this rock has been chosen for making this object.

- Bring your picture and information to class.

This activity is a good way to demonstrate the Science in Context objective: 6SIC.02 Describe how science is used in their local area

3.4 Soil

LEARNING PLAN

Learning objectives	Learning intention	Success criteria
6ESp.03 Know that there are different types of soils and they can be classified based on their clay, sand and organic content.	• Find out that there are different types of soils and they can be classified based on their clay, sand and organic content.	• Learners can find out that there are different types of soils and they can be classified based on their clay, sand and organic content.
6ESp.04 Know that soil composition can change, which can support, or hinder, plant growth.	• Find out that the composition of soil can change making it better or worse for plants to grow in it.	• Learners can find out that the composition of soil can change making it better or worse for plants to grow in it.
6TWSp.03 Make predictions, referring to relevant scientific knowledge and understanding within familiar and unfamiliar contexts.	• Make a prediction and see whether observation supports your prediction.	• Learners can make a prediction about what soil contains.

CONTINUED

Learning objectives	Learning intention	Success criteria
6TWSc.01 Sort, group and classify objects, materials and living things through testing, observation and using secondary information.	• Observe and sort different materials in soil.	• Learners can observe and sort different materials in soil.
6TWSc.08 Collect and record observations and/or measurements in tables and diagrams appropriate to the type of scientific enquiry.	• Record observations in a table.	• Learners can record observations in a table.
6TWSa.01 Describe the accuracy of predictions, based on results.	• Describe the accuracy of predictions, based on results.	• Learners can describe the accuracy of predictions, based on results.

LANGUAGE SUPPORT

Learners will use the following words:

soil: a mixture of broken up rocks, organic matter, water and air

texture: the feel of a material, e.g. rough or smooth

organic matter: living things or things which were alive, such as dead leaves, bits of root and twigs

loam: a soil with a balance of sand, clay and organic matter

waterlogged: full of water that will not drain through

nutrients: food in the form of organic matter and minerals such as iron and phosphates. In this topic we look at nutrients for plants. Many humans also take in extra nutrients in the form of vitamin pills

compost: a natural fertiliser made of dead organic matter such as dead leaves and insects

artificial fertiliser: a fertiliser is a mixture of organic matter and minerals that help plants to grow. An artificial fertiliser is a factory-made fertiliser made from chemicals

pesticide: a factory-made product that kills unwanted insects but also kills the organic matter in the soil

composition: what something is made or consists of. In this topic we talk about soil composition which means describing what soil consists of.

In English we also talk about musical compositions and compositions as works of art.

Starter ideas

1 Getting started (10 minutes)

Resources: Learner's Book

Description: Tell learners to look at the photograph. Ask them the questions in the Learner's Book.

1   They should know that the vegetables are growing in soil.

2   Rock – this is the Earth's crust.

3   This revises what they learnt in Topic 3.2 – weathering breaks up rock by heating and cooling and with water and ice. They will see that the broken up rocks form soil.

2 What does a plant grow in? (10 minutes)

Resources: Bring a pot plant to class

Description: Ask learners:

What is the plant growing in? (Soil)

Why does the plant need soil to grow?

(Soil gives a base for the roots to hold on to as the plant grows bigger; the plant takes up water through the soil; the plant takes up food/nutrients through the soil.)

Main teaching ideas

1 Think like a scientist: Investigate a soil sample (45 minutes)

Learning intentions: Make a prediction and see whether observation supports your prediction.

Observe and sort different materials in soil.

Record observations in a table.

Resources: Learner's Book

For each group: a tin or jar of soil – make sure there is some organic matter in the soil and, if possible, some insects such ants or worms, a few sheets of newspaper or plastic sheet to cover the desk.

If you have a tap nearby, learners can wash their hands after handling the soil. Otherwise have some wet wipes ready to hand out.

Description: Learners should begin by drawing the table in their notebooks ready to put their observations in.

Then learners work in groups to do steps 1–4.

They must use the questions 1–10 to help them to observe the soil.

Record their observations in the table.

> **Practical guidance:** Divide class into groups of 4–5 learners.

Each group can work at one desk. Cover the desk with newspaper or a plastic sheet.

Walk around the class and help where necessary.

Make sure everyone feels the soil in order to describe the texture.

When learners have finished they must put the soil back in the tin or jar because they will look at it again in the next section. Label the tins/jars with groups' names and store them in the classroom. Make sure they tidy their desk and wash or wet wipe

their hands before you continue with the lesson.

> **Differentiation ideas:** Try to mix abilities in each group.

> **Assessment ideas:** This is a good opportunity for learners to assess their group skills. They can answer the questions in 'How am I doing?'

2 Types of soil (30 minutes)

Learning intention: Find out that there are different types of soils and they can be classified based on their clay, sand and organic content.

Observe and sort different materials in soil.

Record results in a table.

Resources: Learner's Book

Soil samples from the previous section, a bottle of water, wet wipes or water to wash hands

Description: Ask learners: *Where do the particles that make up soil come from?* (Rocks)

Then ask learners: *Do you think different rocks can make different soils?* (Yes)

Read aloud the paragraphs under Types of soil. This forms a good link with the earlier topics on different types of rock.

Then read aloud the sections on Sandy soil and Clay soil. Compare the photographs and the diagrams which show the different textures of these soils.

Ask the learners if they have seen water that does not drain away on top of fields or gardens. This shows that the soil is waterlogged and that it is likely to be clay soil.

Then read the section on Loam. This type of soil has the best composition – a mixture of sand and clay and organic matter.

Finish this section by telling learners to answer questions 2 and 3 in Activity 1: Types of soil. Learners should then get into the groups they were in for the first part of the topic. They re-visit their soil sample and decide whether it is a sandy, clay or loam soil to answer question 1.

> **Practical guidance:** You will need the soil samples you used earlier in the topic, some newspaper or plastic sheets. Each group can work at one desk. Cover the desk with newspaper or a plastic sheet.

They will need some water to test how well the soil holds water.

Make sure they tidy their desk and wash or wet wipe their hands before you continue with the lesson.

They do not need to use the soil again so you can put the soil in the nearest garden.

> **Assessment ideas:** Go through the answers in class before moving on to the next section.

3 Changing the composition of soil (30 minutes)

Learning intentions: Find out that the composition of soil can change, making it better or worse for plants to grow in.

Record observations in a table.

Resources: Learner's Book; Digital Classroom video: Compost (optional)

Description: Ask learners if they have a garden or allotment or if they know someone who has one. Does the gardener add anything to the soil?

Do you know what they add? Why do they add things to the soil?

Learners may know that it is important to add compost or fertilisers to the soil. Otherwise, once the plants have used up the nutrients in the soil they will not grow so well and could die.

Sometimes people add lime to the soil if the soil contains too much acid. The lime neutralises or cancels out the acid to make the soil more balanced.

Read aloud the sections on Compost and Damaging soil.

Ask learners if they make compost at home, or if they know anyone that does. Share with the class how they make the compost.

> **Digital Classroom:** If you have access to the Digital Classroom component, show the video 'Compost'. The i button will explain how to use the video.

Ask learners how gardeners get rid of pests like snails. Some people pick up the snails and get rid of them. Others use snail bait, but this can poison the fruits on the plants as well as the snails. Some people have home remedies for getting rid of garden pests. Share these in class.

To consolidate this section, Learners should answer the questions in Activity 2: Changing the composition of soil in their notebooks.

> **Assessment ideas:** Ask learners to compare their answers in class.

4 Looking after pot plants (15 minutes)

Learning intention: Find out that the composition of soil can change making it better or worse for plants to grow in.

Resources: Tips for a healthy pot plant:

- Put holes in the bottom of the pot and water the pot often.

- Use potting soil from a garden shop. This soil contains nutrients. Continue to feed your plant with nutrients every two weeks.

Description: Give learners the information above. Answer these questions:

1 Why do you have to make holes in the bottom of the pot?

2 Why do you need to water the plant often?

3 What are nutrients?

4 How does soil in a pot change over time?

Differentiation: Many learners will have pot plants at home, so they will feel confident to answer these questions.

Answers

1 To allow the water to drain through/so that the soil does not become waterlogged.

2 Because the water drains through the soil quickly.

3 Food for plants such as organic matter and minerals such as iron and phosphates.

4 It becomes dried out and infertile as all the nutrients are absorbed by the plant.

> **Assessment ideas:** Ask learners to compare their answers in class.

Plenary ideas

1 Workbook: Challenge exercise (15 minutes)

Resources: Workbook

Description: Read the case study about Organic Farming aloud. Then get different learners to read it. Discuss words learners do not know. This information will make a good ending by showing how farmers can maintain the composition of their soil and also make food healthier for consumers.

Learners can answer the questions for homework if you are running out of time.

> **Assessment ideas:** Go through the answers in class.

> **Reflection ideas:** See the Learner's Book:

How can you use what you have found out in this topic to look after soil in the future?

2 Workbook: Focus exercise (10 minutes)

Resources: Workbook

Description: Learners answer questions in the Workbook.

> **Assessment ideas:** Learners can swap with a partner and mark each other's work.

Homework ideas

1 Workbook: Focus, Practice and/or Challenge exercises.

The Focus and Practice exercises are straightforward and suitable for all learners. Go through the answers to the questions in your next lesson.

If you started the Challenge activity in class, learners can answer the questions for homework.

2 Worksheet 3.4.

This is based on a case study about an African farming family and how they look after the soil. See below for details.

3 Find out which soils are best for growing rice and maize and compare them.

Answers

Rice in monsoon areas is grown in clay loam soil or silty clay. Maize grows best in well-drained soil such as sandy loam.

Topic Worksheets

Worksheet 3.4: Soil: Case study

The first page contains a case study about an African farming family – all learners will need to read this before they go on to answer the questions on one of the three worksheets.

- Worksheet 3.4A – has questions where learners have to supply missing words in the answers.

- Worksheet 3.4B – learners have to write full sentences for their answers.

- Worksheet 3.4C – learners have to present their answers in a table.

PROJECT: HOW PEOPLE USE SOIL

6SIC.02 Describe how science is used in their local area.
6SIC.04 Identify people who use science, including professionally, in their area and describe how they use science.

Advise learners to do their interview in pairs or small groups. They may have to be accompanied by an older sibling or relative.

They should write out their questions beforehand, leaving spaces to write in answers.

It may be better to speak to the person in their own language and then translate the information into English.

Each learner should produce their own poster for assessment.

The poster need not be bigger than A4 size.

Display the completed posters in the classroom.

Assessment rubric

Here is a rubric you could use to assess the posters. Or you could give this rubric to the class and get them to assess the posters.

Mark out of 10	Description of poster
8–10	Eye-catching, imaginative, colourful, well illustrated, interesting information
6–7	Eye-catching, colourful, plenty of information
5	Not very eye-catching, pictures and information but not very interesting
3–4	Not eye-catching, not enough information or pictures
1–2	Little or no information or effort.

> 4 Food chains and food webs

Unit plan

Topic	Approx. number of learning hours	Outline of learning content	Resources
4.1 Food chains, food webs and energy transfers	1.5–2	• Identify food chains in food webs. • Trace pathway of energy from producers to consumers.	**Learner's Book:** Activity: Draw food chains Think like a scientist: Explain a food web and draw food chains **Workbook:** Topic 4.1 **Digital Classroom:** Video – Feeding levels in a food chain Animation – Food chains Song – Food chains
4.2 Harm to food chains and food webs	2–3	• Harmful substances can move through food chains and food webs.	**Learner's Book:** Think like a scientist: Play a food chain game Activity: Research information about mercury in food chains **Workbook:** Topic 4.2 ⤓ Worksheet 4.2

Across unit resources
Learner's Book: Project: Reducing plastics in food chains
Check your progress quiz
Teacher's Resource:
⤓ Language worksheets 1 & 2
⤓ Diagnostic test
⤓ Mid-year test
⤓ End-of-year test
⤓ End-of-unit test
Digital Classroom:
End-of-unit quiz

BACKGROUND KNOWLEDGE

Food webs

Learners should already know that plants produce their own food using energy from the Sun and are, therefore, known as producers. Animals eat or consume plants and other animals to obtain the energy they need. Animals are, therefore, consumers. Food chains show the direction of energy transfer from one living thing to another. A food chain is a drawing representing feeding relationships and energy transfers between living things.

However, the transfer of energy in ecosystems is much more complex than in a single food chain. Most consumers eat more than one other species of plant or animal. Producers are usually eaten by many different herbivores or omnivores. Most herbivores are eaten by more than one carnivore or omnivore. A food web shows all the possible food chains a living thing can be part of in its habitat and is, therefore, a more accurate representation of energy transfers between organisms.

Each feeding level in a food chain is known as a trophic level. Energy transfers between trophic levels in food chains and food webs are not efficient. On average, only about 10% of the energy present in one trophic level is transferred to the next trophic level. The remaining 90% of the energy moves out of the food

chain to the surroundings as heat or is used by the organism itself for growth, movement, reproduction and other life processes. As a result of the decreasing quantity of energy available to each successive trophic level, there are usually no more than five trophic levels in food chains. There are also fewer individuals at the end of food chains, for the same reason.

Threats to food chains and food webs from toxic substances

Polluting chemicals sometimes enter food chains, either accidently in the case of spills, or on purpose, such as with fertilisers and pesticides. Many of these substances are harmful or toxic. Some toxic chemicals break down into harmless substances in the environment. Others are persistent and do not break down naturally, for example microplastics, heavy metals such as mercury and lead, and some pesticides. These chemicals remain in the environment for a very long time. They get absorbed by organisms at the bottom of the food chains and build up at higher levels because they are not broken down in the bodies of living organisms. Predators at the end of the food chain are affected most as the levels of toxic substances are highest in their trophic level of the chain.

TEACHING SKILLS FOCUS

Reflective teaching

In each topic of the Learner's Book, learners have the opportunity to reflect on their learning and to think about what they are pleased with and how they could do things differently next time in order to improve their learning. The reflection process can also be valuable for teachers to consider what they do in the classroom, think about why they do it and it if works.

The process of reflective teaching is an ongoing one with four steps:

1 Teach

2 Consider the effect of your teaching on learning. For example:
   - What made the lesson go well? Why was it successful?

   - If the learners didn't understand an explanation, why was is it unclear? Is there a better way of getting the idea across?
   - If learners misbehaved, what were they doing and why?

3 Consider different ways of teaching to improve the quality of learning, for example:
   - creating more opportunities for hands-on work
   - allowing learners to explain new ideas to one another to help them explore their own understanding of the concepts.

4 Try out your ideas.
   There are various ways to start a process of reflection.
   - Teacher diary: after each lesson, write in a notebook what happened in the lesson.

CONTINUED

- Recording lessons: with permission from your school and parents, you could make video or audio recordings of lessons. Use these to look for things you do in class that you are not aware of or things happening that you do not normally see.
- Learner feedback: ask learners for their opinions and perceptions. This can be done with simple questionnaires, for example:
  - What did you like most/least about this lesson?
  - What helped you to learn in this lesson?
  - What would you like to change in the lesson?
- Two column notes: in the first column, ask yourself questions about what happened in the lesson. In the second column, write questions about what these things mean for your teaching. For example:

Column 1: What happened?	Column 2: What does this mean?
What went well today?	How can I make it happen again? What could I improve on next time?
Did learners achieve today's success criteria?	How do I know?
How did learners respond to the lesson?	How will this change tomorrow's lesson?
Why was today's lesson important?	How will learners use this in their lives?
What was the most challenging thing that happened today?	How will I respond next time?

Challenge yourself to try the reflection process at least once in every topic of the unit.

4.1 Food chains, food webs and energy transfers

LEARNING PLAN

Learning objectives	Learning intention	Success criteria
6Be.01 Interpret food webs and identify food chains within them.	• To draw food chains. • To explain a food web and identify food chains in a food web.	• Learners can draw food chains. • Learners can explain a food web and identify food chains in a food web.
6Be.03 Identify the energy source of a food chain/web and describe how energy is transferred through a food chain/web.	• To identify the source of energy in food chains and food webs. • to describe how energy is transferred in food chains and food webs.	• Learners can identify the source of energy in food chains and food webs. • Learners can describe how energy is transferred in food chains and food webs.
6TWSm.01 Describe how a model can help us understand and describe scientific phenomena and ideas.	• To explain how a food web shows feeding relationships in nature.	• Learners can explain how a food web shows feeding relationships in nature.
6TWSm.02 Use models, including diagrams, to represent and describe scientific phenomena and ideas.	• To draw food chains that represent energy transfers and feeding relationships in nature.	• Learners can draw food chains that represent energy transfers and feeding relationships in nature.

LANGUAGE SUPPORT

Learners will use the following words:

food chain: a drawing that shows the order in which animals eat plants and other animals to get energy

food web: a drawing of a number of linked food chains

accurate: correct and true, more real, without mistakes, for example, Zola's calculations were very accurate

represent: to show or stand for, for example, the colour red usually represents danger. It can also mean to act in place of, for example, Mr Singh will represent his town at the meeting.

Give learners the opportunity to use these words correctly by asking them to write or complete sentences using the words. Sentences made with everyday words do not have to be scientific.

Common misconceptions

Misconception	How to identify	How to overcome
Food chain arrows represent who eats whom rather than flow of energy.	Ask learners why living things eat other living things.	Explain that living things eat other living things in order to get the energy they need to live. A food chain is a drawing that shows the order in which energy passes from one living thing to another in the food it eats.
Predators are big, ferocious, wild animals such as lions and tigers.	Show learners pictures of predators, some big, such as a crocodile or tiger, and some small, such as a spider, ladybird or frog. Ask learners to identify the predators. Ask them why they say the animal is a predator.	Explain that a predator is any animal that kills and eats other animals.

Starter ideas

1 Getting started (10–15 minutes)

Resources: Learner's Book, Venn diagram template

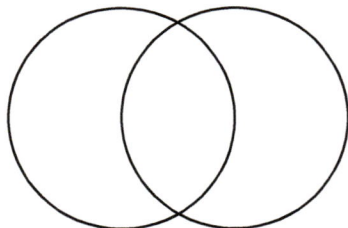

Description: This activity draws on learners' existing knowledge about producers and consumers.

Tell learners to work in pairs to read and answer the questions in the Learner's Book. Give each pair a Venn diagram template.

You can ask learners to put up their hands to volunteer to share their answers and show their Venn diagrams.

2 Feeding relationships in nature (10–15 minutes)

Resources: Digital Classroom video: Feeding levels in a food chain (optional) or video clips showing herbivores, omnivores and carnivores eating and catching food.

Description

› **Digital Classroom:** If you have access to the Digital Classroom component, show the video 'Feeding levels in a food chain'. The i button will explain how to use the video. Then show it again and pause between clips. Ask learners to identify the herbivores, omnivores, carnivores, producers, predators and prey they see. Alternatively, do an internet search for video clips showing herbivores, omnivores and carnivores eating and catching food.

Learners' answers will help you identify the misconception that all predators are large and fierce.

Main teaching ideas

1 Activity: Draw food chains (10–15 minutes)

Learning intentions: To draw food chains

Resources: Learner's Book

Digital Classroom animation: Food chains (optional)

Digital Classroom song: Food chains (optional)

Description: Remind learners that we show the direction in which energy passes in the food that living things eat in a drawing called a food chain.

> **Digital Classroom:** If you have access to the Digital Classroom component, show learners the animation 'Food chains' as well as the song 'Food chains'. The i button will explain how to use the animation and song.

Ask learners to draw a food chain of their own.

Remind them of the direction in which the energy moves: plant/producer → herbivore → carnivore.

Then let them work individually to draw the food chains in the activity.

> **Differentiation ideas:** Challenge more confident learners to draw a food chain with five links. Note that links are plants or animals, not the arrow between them.

> **Assessment ideas:** Discuss answers in class and allow learners to check their own work and make any corrections needed.

2 Think like a scientist: Explain a food web and draw food chains (15–20 minutes)

Learning intentions: To explain a food web and identify food chains in a food web.

To explain how a food web shows feeding relationships in nature.

To draw food chains that represent energy transfers and feeding relationships in nature.

Resources: Learner's Book

Description: Tell learners to study the food web in the Learner's Book. They can work in pairs to answer the questions.

> **Differentiation ideas:** Less confident learners can draw three columns in their notebooks. As they study the food web, they should note whether each living thing eats plants, animals or both and then write the living thing's name in the appropriate column. This more systematic approach will make it easier to identify the different feeding types.

As a challenge, more confident learners can count the total number of food chains in the food web.

> **Assessment ideas:** Learners can answer the self-assessment questions in the How am I doing? feature in the Learner's Book.

3 Demonstrate energy transfers in food chains and food webs (10 minutes)

Learning intentions: To describe how energy is transferred in food chains and food webs.

Resources: 100 marbles, buttons, sweets or paper tokens

Description: The marbles, buttons, sweets or paper tokens represent energy. Learners will make a food chain and pass on the marbles, buttons, sweets or paper tokens to the living things in the food chain in order.

You can encourage learners to act out their food chains.

At each energy transfer they will see that most of the energy is not passed on to the next living thing in the food chain, but is used by the plant or animal itself or transferred to the environment.

Ask learners these questions:

Why do you think there are usually not more than four or five links in a food chain?

Why there are fewer carnivores than herbivores in a habitat?

> **Practical guidance:** Learners should work in groups of five to form food chains. Each group should have a 'Sun', a 'producer', a 'herbivore' and a 'carnivore'. The fifth person represents the 'environment'.

Tell learners to decide which living things are part of their food chain, e.g. corn, a mouse and an owl.

The Sun must give the 'producer' the 100 marbles, buttons, sweets or paper tokens. The 'herbivore' should pretend to eat the 'producer'. The 'producer' must give 10 marbles, buttons, sweets or paper tokens to the 'herbivore', keep 50 for itself and give 40 to the 'environment'.

Next, the 'carnivore' must catch and eat the 'herbivore'. The 'herbivore' must give 1 marble, button, sweet or paper counter to the 'herbivore', keep 5 for itself and give 4 to the 'environment'.

Learners will observe that only a small part of the energy present at the start of the food chain is eventually transferred to the last living thing in the chain.

Answers

Learners should be able to explain that only about 10% of the energy the producer obtains from the Sun is transferred to the next link in the food chain, the herbivore. The carnivore receives 10% of the energy the herbivore obtained from the producer. So less and less energy is available to animals at higher levels in the food chain. This means that food chains cannot be very long or there would be too little energy for the animals at the end of the food chain.

There are fewer carnivores than herbivores in a habitat because when a herbivore eats, most of the energy it obtains from the plants it eats is used up by the herbivore itself to carry out its own life processes or is transferred to the environment, mainly as heat. So very little of the energy is stored in its body. Therefore, a carnivore has to eat many herbivores to get sufficient energy to survive and grow.

> **Differentiation ideas:** Draw or show a picture of an energy pyramid which illustrates the relative quantity of energy on each feeding level in a food chain to learners who struggle to grasp the idea of energy losses in a food chain. This is a useful visual aid to show how the quantity of energy decreases on successive levels of the food chain.

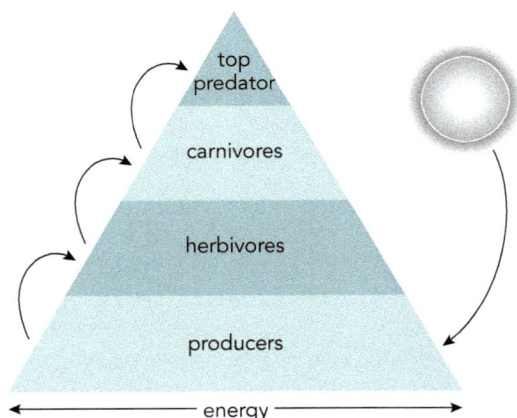

> **Assessment ideas:** Ask learners to answer these self-assessment questions:

Do I understand how energy is transferred in a food chain?

Can I explain what happens to the energy in each link of a food chain?

Do I understand why food chains do not have very many links?

They can draw a green dot next to the questions for which their answer is 'yes', a yellow dot next to the questions for which their answer is 'sort of' and a red dot next the questions for which their answer is 'no'. Follow up on learners who draw yellow and red dots and give them additional help and support.

Plenary ideas

1 What have you learnt? (5 minutes)

Description: Let learners stand and quickly say one thing that they have learnt in the topic before sitting down. You will probably not have time for all learners to give an answer, so choose or ask five or six learners to volunteer their ideas.

> **Assessment ideas:** Learners' answers should give you a quick overview of how well the class has understood the work covered in the topic.

2 Tell the teacher (5–10 minutes)

Resources: Set of questions (see below)

Description: Make a set of questions to give to learners to answer about their feelings about the lesson or topic. Some examples are:

- What did you like most about this lesson?
- What did you like least about this lesson?
- What helped you to learn in this lesson?
- What would you like to change in the lesson?

Learners' answers will help you reflect on your teaching and possibly consider trying other strategies or approaches.

> **Reflection ideas:** Learners can answer the Reflection questions at the end of the topic in the Learner's Book.

CROSS-CURRICULAR LINKS

Drawing a Venn diagram in Starter idea 1 can be linked with Maths. Venn diagrams are used in Stage 4 Maths to sort data and objects using two or three criteria.

Reading and following written instructions for activities in the Learner's Book and writing answer sentences to questions in the Learner's Book can be linked with comprehension skills and sentence construction in English.

Making a food web, as suggested for Homework idea 1, can be linked with Arts and Crafts.

Homework ideas

1 Learners can make their own food webs. They should find and cut out pictures of different plants and animals to make a food web that contains at least four food chains. They can also draw pictures if they wish to. Learners should glue the pictures onto card or paper and use lengths of wool or string to connect the different plants and animals in the food chains.

In the next lesson, allow learners to display their food webs and explain them to other learners.

2 Learners could complete the Focus, Practice and/ or Challenge Workbook Exercises for the topic, depending on their progress.

In the next lesson, discuss answers in class.

Allow learners to check their own work.

4.2 Harm to food chains and food webs

LEARNING PLAN

Learning objectives	Learning intention	Success criteria
6Be.02 Know that some substances can be toxic and damage living things, and that these substances can move through a food chain/web.	• To learn that some substances can harm living things, and that these substances can move through a food chain or food web.	• Learners can understand that some substances can harm living things, and that these substances can move through a food chain or food web.
6TWSm.01 Describe how a model can help us understand and describe scientific phenomena and ideas.	• To explain how a game can show the way harmful substances can move through a food chain or food web.	• Learners can explain how a game can show how harmful substances can move through a food chain or food web.
6TWSm.02 Use models, including diagrams, to represent and describe scientific phenomena and ideas.	• To play a game to show how harmful substances can move through a food chain or food web.	• Learners can play a game to show how harmful substances can move through a food chain or food web.
6TWSc.08 Collect and record observations and/or measurements in tables and diagrams appropriate to the type of scientific enquiry.	• To record results in a table.	• Learners can record results in a table.
6TWSa.05 Present and interpret results using tables, bar charts, dot plots, line graphs and scatter graphs.	• To draw a graph of results.	• Learners can draw a graph of results.
6TWSa.02 Describe patterns in results, including identifying any anomalous results.	• To describe a pattern in results.	• Learners can describe a pattern in results.
6TWSc.07 Use a range of secondary information sources to research and select relevant evidence to answer questions.	• To research information to answer questions about a harmful substance in food chains.	• Learners can research information to answer questions about a harmful substance in food chains.

LANGUAGE SUPPORT

The key terms for this topic are:

toxic: harmful or poisonous, for example, the factory produced toxic gases

microplastics: very small particles of plastic that make their way into the environment, especially rivers and seas

pesticides: chemicals that farmers spray on their crops to kill pests, such as insects and snails

environment: the air, water, land and living things around us. It can also refer to the general surroundings or conditions where people, animals

and plants live, for example, a dirty kitchen is an unhealthy environment

accumulate: to increase in quantity over time. For example, the runner accumulated a big collection of medals over the years

Make a classroom glossary board with new words and their meanings that learners can look at if they are unsure of a word's meaning. You could also write how the word sounds next to each term, for example, 'peh-stuh-side' (pesticide) next to the word definition.

Common misconceptions

Misconception	How to identify	How to overcome
If water is clear, it is safe to drink and safe for other living things.	Show pictures of clean water and dirty or muddy water. Ask which one is safe to drink. Learners will probably say it is the clear water.	Take a beaker of water and add some of hydrochloric acid to it. Tell learners you are adding acid. Is the water safe to drink? Would learners know if the water was safe to drink or not just by looking at it?

Starter ideas

1 Getting started (10–15 minutes)

Resources: Learner's Book

Description: This activity draws on learners' existing knowledge about things that can harm living organisms in food chains and food webs.

Tell learners to read the instructions in the Learner's Book.

Learners should work in groups to draw mind maps and then explain their mind map to another group. You can ask learners to put up their hands to volunteer to share one thing they think is harmful to living things in food chains and food webs. Record answers on the board in a class mind map and discuss them.

2 Harmful substances in food chains (10–15 minutes)

Resources: Video/s from the internet

Description: Use search terms such as 'DDT/pesticides/microplastics in food chains' to look for videos on the internet that show how these substances enter food chains and can harm living things.

At the end of the video, ask learners questions such as:

Which substance was harmful?

Where did it come from?

How did it get into the food chain or food web?

How did the substance harm living things in the food chain or food web?

Discuss answer as a class. Learners' answers will depend on the video/s they have seen.

This activity addresses the Science in Context strand in the curriculum.

Main teaching ideas

1 The plastic problem (10–15 minutes)

Learning intention: To demonstrate that some substances do not break down completely in the environment.

Resources: A sheet of plastic wrap or other plastic

Per pair: a sheet of thin paper such as tissue paper or tracing paper, scissors

Description: Learners should work in pairs. Ask learners how many of them have used something plastic today. Ask what happens to plastics we don't want.

Explain that plastics never disappear, they just break down into smaller and smaller pieces.

Ask what learners think would happen if these tiny bits of plastic got into a river or the sea. Would the animals living there be able to see the bits so they could avoid swallowing them? Would the animals think the plastic bits were food particles? What would happen if the animals swallowed the pieces of plastic?

Explain that aquatic animals such as fish, jelly fish and shrimps mistake tiny plastic particles for food. Once inside the body, the plastics do not disappear. They stay in the body and are passed on when another animal (or person) eats the fish or jellyfish that has swallowed the plastic. Some plastics have harmful effects inside the body.

> **Practical guidance:** Learners should work in pairs.

Demonstrate the idea that plastics break down into smaller and smaller pieces by cutting a piece of plastic into as many small pieces as you can. Make sure you dispose of the cut-up plastic pieces safely.

Then tell learners to cut the sheet of paper into the smallest pieces they can. Explain that they are using paper as it is much less harmful to the environment than plastic when we throw it away.

> **Assessment ideas:** Get pairs of learners to write down any two things they learnt from doing the activity and to share them with another pair.

2   **Think like a scientist: Play a food chain game (30–40 minutes)**

Learning intentions: To play a game to show how harmful substances can move through a food chain or food web.

To explain how a game can show the way harmful substances can move through a food chain or food web.

To record results in a table.

To draw a graph of results.

To describe a pattern in results.

Resources: Learner's Book

Paper cups marked with different colours, chalk, paper pesticide 'particles', sticky notes or pieces of sticky putty

Description: Tell learners they are going to play a game to model how a pesticide moves through and

accumulates in a food chain. Read through the instructions in the Learner's Book with the class to make sure they know how the game works.

If learners do not know how to calculate an average, explain that they should add up the number of particles each person collects in their cup and divide the total by the number of people on that level of the food chain.

> **Practical guidance:**

1   Cut up paper to make about 100 pesticide 'particles'. This should be enough for a class size of up to 30 learners. Make more if you have a bigger class.

2   Mark off a game area with chalk. Use an area large enough for learners to move quickly, possibly a school hall or gym. Spread the pesticide 'particles' around the entire game area.

3   Divide up learners into rice plants, caterpillars, frogs and kingfishers. Make sure that the number on each level of the food chain decreases as you go up the food chain. There should be more rice plants than caterpillars, more caterpillars than frogs and more frogs than kingfishers. These are suggested numbers for a class of 30 learners: 14 rice plants, 9 caterpillars, 5 frogs, 2 kingfishers.

4   Mark paper cups with four different colours to show the different levels in the food chain, for example: green = rice plants; yellow = caterpillars; red = frogs; blue = kingfishers. Give each learner a cup according to which living thing in the food chain they represent.

5   Tell learners they must stay within the marked boundary of the playing area. When you give the signal, the 'rice plants' must each pick up as many 'particles' as they can and put them in their cups until all the 'particles' have been collected. 'Rice plants' must count and record in a table the number of 'particles' they have accumulated and put the 'particles' back in the cup.

The 'caterpillars' must tag the 'rice plants' by putting a sticky note or piece of sticky putty on the shoulders of the 'rice plants'. A 'caterpillar' can only tag one 'rice plant' at a time. Continue until all the 'rice plants' are tagged.

The tagged 'rice plants' must put their pesticide 'particles' into the cup of the 'caterpillar' that tagged them.

Whenever any player is tagged or 'eaten', they must empty their cup and sit down.

'Caterpillars' must count and record in a table the number of 'particles' they have accumulated. They must put the 'particles' back into their cups.

'Frogs' must then tag 'caterpillars' and record the number of pesticide 'particles' they have received from the 'caterpillars'.

'Kingfishers' must tag 'frogs' and record the number of pesticide 'particles' they have received from the 'frogs'.

> **Differentiation ideas:** Support less confident learners by discussing the food chain in the game and drawing it on the board so they know which 'living things' to tag/eat.

> **Assessment ideas:** Learners can answer the self-assessment questions in the How are we doing? feature in the Learner's Book.

3   **Activity: Research information about mercury in food chains (20–30 minutes class time for presentations, plus research time at home or in class)**

Learning intentions: To research information to answer questions about a harmful substance in food chains.

Resources: Learner's Book, internet, reference books or encyclopaedias

Description: This activity addresses the Science in Context strand in the curriculum. Tell learners a bit about mercury: it is the only metal that is a liquid at room temperature; it was used in thermometers in the past, but not anymore as is it too dangerous if the thermometers break; it was used in dental fillings until recently; it can combine with other chemicals to form different harmful substances that we cannot see, smell or taste.

Learners should read the instructions in the Learner's Book and work in pairs to research information and prepare their presentations about mercury in food chains. You could allow some class time for this, or else give learners a few days to do the work at home.

> **Differentiation ideas:** Support learners who work more slowly by allowing them more time to prepare their presentations. They can also show you their progress during this time in order for you give them advice and assistance where needed.

> **Assessment ideas:** You could use the following rubric to assess learners' presentations.

Criterion	Poor	Fair	Good	Excellent
Content	Little information provided for each question	Answers some of the questions	Answers all of the questions	Clear and detailed answers to all questions
	No food chain included	Food chain with errors included	Correct food chain included	Correct, detailed food chain included
Visual material used	None/unsuitable/poor quality	Generally suitable, satisfactory quality	Good quality and suitable	Excellent quality and relevant
Overall appearance	Untidy and messy	Fairly tidy and attractive	Neat and attractive	Very neat and attractive

Plenary ideas

1   I can and I know (5–10 minutes)

Resources: Learners will need paper and pens or pencils

Description: This activity does not appear in the Learner's Book.

Ask learners to each write two sentences about what they have learnt in the topic. Their sentences should start with either:

I can …

or

I know …

Give learners one or two minutes to write their sentences. Then write or project a list of success criteria onto the board. Learners can compare their sentences with the success criteria to assess if they have grasped the main ideas and skills covered in the topic.

〉 **Assessment ideas:** This is a self-assessment activity which will help learners to identify areas where they are succeeding or where they need more support.

〉 **Reflection ideas:** Ask learners:

What things did I find easy to learn?

What did I find difficult?

How did I deal with the difficult things?

What would I like to know more about?

2   Talk about it (10–15 minutes)

Resources: A piece of work the learners have completed in the topic.

Description: This activity does not appear in the Learner's Book.

Learners should choose a piece of work they have completed in the topic. They can work in pairs to talk about what they did well in the piece of work and how they think they can improve on it.

〉 **Assessment ideas:** Learners can give each other feedback on their work.

〉 **Reflection ideas:** Learners can answer the Reflection questions in the Learner's Book.

Homework ideas

1   Learners could complete the Focus, Practice and/or Challenge Exercises for the topic in the Workbook, depending on their progress.

In the next lesson, discuss answers. Learners can work in pairs to check one another's answers.

2   Learners could answer the questions at the end of Main teaching idea 2, Think like a scientist: Play a food chain game. Discuss answers in class and allow learners to check their own work and make any corrections needed.

Topic Worksheet

Worksheet 4.2: Make a food web

This worksheet consolidates the main ideas from Topics 4.1 and 4.2. Learners work in groups to construct a food web using themselves and string, and simulate the effects of a harmful substance on the food chain in their food web. You will need to make a set of food web cards to represent the Sun and different plants and animals.

Divide learners into two or three groups of 10 to 15 each. You will need a set of food web cards for each group. Make sure each group has cards to represent the Sun, producers, herbivores and carnivores. There are card templates included with Worksheet 4.2 for you to use.

All learners should be able to complete questions 1–4. Give the Help sheet to learners who need support in working out the order in which the different living things form a food chain. More confident learners can attempt additional questions 5 and 6 on the Stretch sheet.

PROJECT: REDUCING PLASTIC POLLUTION

6SIC.05 Discuss how the use of science and technology can have positive and negative environmental effects on their local area.

6SIC.03 Use science to support points when discussing issues, situations or actions.

Part 1

Learners should work individually to read the information about the ecobrick. They can then get into groups to discuss and answer the questions.

Part 2

Learners should work in pairs to make their product from waste plastic. You could suggest ideas for learners who are struggling to think of what product to make. A plastic scoop or pencil holder are simple products made from plastic bottles. Learners could make flowers or bracelets from plastic bags. They will also find lots of ideas on the internet.

Assessment rubric

Learners can assess their peers' products using a checklist as follows

	Yes	Partly	No
Is the product made from waste plastics?			
Does the information sheet explain what the product is?			
Does the information sheet say how the product was made?			
Does the information sheet say how the product helps the environment			
Does the product look neat and well-made?			

>5 Forces and electricity

Unit plan

Topic	Approx. number of learning hours	Outline of learning content	Resources
5.1 Mass and weight	2	• Find out the difference between mass and weight and compare mass and weight of objects by measuring. • Find out how astronauts cope with weightlessness in space.	**Learner's Book:** Activity 1: What is the difference between mass and weight? Think like a scientist: Measure the mass and weight of objects Activity 2: How gravity affects weight in space **Workbook:** Topic 5.1 ⬇ Worksheets 5.1A, 5.1B and 5.1C **Digital Classroom:** Video – Missions to the Moon
5.2 The effects of forces	2	• Investigate the effects of different forces on a ball at rest and in motion.	**Learner's Book:** Think like a scientist: Investigate and discuss the effects of forces on an object Activity 1: The effects of forces Activity 2: Identify the effects of forces in ball games **Workbook:** Topic 5.2 **Digital Classroom:** Activity – Effect of forces
5.3 Floating and sinking	3	• Discuss the concepts of floating and sinking and carry out investigations to see how mass affects floating and sinking and how shape affects floating and sinking.	**Learner's Book:** Think like a scientist 1: How does mass affect floating and sinking? Activity: Fair testing, force diagrams and writing a conclusion Think like a scientist 2: How does shape affect floating and sinking? **Workbook:** Topic 5.2 **Digital Classroom:** Video – Archimedes and displacement

Topic	Approx. number of learning hours	Outline of learning content	Resources
5.4 Different circuits and circuit diagrams	3	• Use circuit symbols to draw circuit diagrams and read circuit diagrams. Build a circuit with a buzzer and build and compare a series and a parallel circuit.	**Learner's Book:** Activity: Use circuit symbols to read and draw circuit diagrams Think like a scientist 1: Build circuits with different components Think like a scientist 2: Make and compare a series circuit and a parallel circuit **Workbook:** Topic 5 ⬇ Worksheet 5.4 **Digital Classroom:** Activity – Circuit symbols

Across unit resources		
Learner's Book: Project: Rechargeable batteries Check your progress quiz	**Teacher's Resource:** ⬇ Language worksheets 1 & 2 ⬇ Diagnostic test ⬇ Mid-year test ⬇ End-of-year test ⬇ End-of-unit test	**Digital Classroom:** End-of-unit quiz

BACKGROUND KNOWLEDGE

In this unit there are several topics which you need to treat carefully to avoid misconceptions.

In Topic 5.1 you introduce the idea that mass and weight are different. This is difficult because in everyday life we talk about the weight of an object in kg when scientifically it is mass that is measured in kg. However, the idea that your weight would be different on the Moon or another planet but your mass remains the same should capture learners' interest.

Another topic where misconceptions easily happen is 5.3: Floating and sinking. Most learners will think that heavy objects sink and light objects float… but then you look at the picture of the huge heavy container ship floating! The key to this lies in density – mass per unit volume – which learners will not come across until Stage 7. Objects with tightly packed molecules are denser and will sink. Objects with more loosely packed molecules are less dense and will float. Objects float depending on their density compared to water; for an object to float its density needs to be less than that of water. However, in Stage 6 learners go part of the way to

understanding floating and sinking. They will find out that for a given container that floats, increasing the mass will eventually cause the container to sink. They also discover that by making the surface area of an object larger you can increase the mass of the load more before it sinks.

Towards the end of the topic we introduce the idea of adding air to an object to make it float. Objects float when air is enclosed in an object because their density is lowered, thereby increasing the likelihood of floating.

In Topic 5.4 learners extend their knowledge of electricity. They learn how to understand and draw circuit diagrams. Allow learners to use the table of conventional symbols while they practise identifying circuit diagrams and drawing their own. The more they practise, the sooner they will remember the symbols. Learners are introduced to parallel circuits for the first time. This is a step closer to understanding how electricity is supplied to homes – parallel circuits allow us to switch on a lamp or an appliance in one room without all the lamps and appliances in other rooms coming on.

TEACHING SKILLS FOCUS

Group work

In this unit there are several opportunities for group work. The Think like a scientist activities in Topics 5.2 and 5.3 do not require scientific apparatus, so learners should definitely do these activities in groups.

You can either choose who should go into each group or allow learners to choose their own group. The size of the group will depend on how many learners you have in the class and what resources you have available. A good group size is 4–6 learners – more than that will mean some learners may not participate.

Make sure every member of the group has a particular responsibility. For example, in Think like a scientist 1: How does mass affect floating and sinking? in Topic 5.3, you could divide the tasks as follows:

- Learner 1: draws the table and enters the predictions and results.
- Learner 2: Keeps time. Their job is to monitor progress and keep the group within the time frame you have given them.
- Learner 3: Half-fills the container with water and is in charge of steadying the small container.

- Learner 4: Measures 10 g of sand each time (or you can use flour or rice).
- Learner 5: Puts the sand into the container.
- All learners combine efforts to tidy up when finished.

For the next activity, learners could keep to the same group but swap roles.

Group work is an important way of learning not only science skills, such as measuring, recording results and fair testing, but also life skills because it encourages the following:

- interaction and working together
- discussion and communication skills
- time management
- responsibility
- strategies for dealing with conflict
- helping each other.

Make an effort to get your class to do several activities in groups during the course of this unit. The more you do this, the better your groups' organising skills will become.

5.1 Mass and weight

LEARNING PLAN

Learning objectives	Learning intention	Success criteria
6Pf.01 Describe the difference between mass, measured in kilograms (kg), and weight, measured in newtons (N).	• Describe the difference between mass, measured in kilograms (kg), and weight, measured in newtons (N).	• Learners can describe the difference between mass measured in kilograms (kg) and weight measured in newtons (N).
6Pf.02 Describe the effect of gravity and know that when gravity changes, the weight of an object changes but the mass does not.	• Describe the effect of gravity and know that when gravity changes, the weight of an object changes but the mass does not.	• Learners can understand how gravity affects weight. • Learners can know that when gravity changes, weight changes but mass does not.

CONTINUED

Learning objectives	Learning intention	Success criteria
6TWSp.02 Know the features of the five main types of scientific enquiry.	• Practise pattern seeking.	• Learners can practise pattern seeking.
6TWSc.04 Decide when measurements need to be repeated to give more reliable data.	• Decide when it is necessary to repeat measurements to give more reliable data.	• Learners can repeat measurements when results do not fit the pattern.
6TWSc.05 Take appropriately accurate measurements.	• Measure the mass and weight of objects.	• Learners can measure the mass and weight of objects.
6TWSa.02 Describe patterns in results, including identifying any anomalous results.	• Describe a pattern in results and identify any results that do not fit the pattern.	• Learners can describe a pattern in results and identify any results that do not fit the pattern.
6TWSa.03 Make a conclusion from results informed by scientific understanding.	• Make a conclusion from results using science knowledge.	• Learners can make a conclusion from results using science knowledge.
6TWSa.05 Present and interpret results using tables, bar charts, dot plots, line graphs and scatter graphs.	• Record measurements in a table.	• Learners can record measurements in a table.

LANGUAGE SUPPORT

Learners will use the following words:

mass: the quantity of matter in an object. Mass is measured in kilograms (kg)

This will probably make more sense when learners find out more about matter and what it contains (atoms and molecules) in a later stage.

The word 'mass' is used in everyday English to mean a large number, for example a mass of people. It is also the name of the service in a Catholic church.

weight: the force of attraction on an object caused by gravity. Weight is measured in newtons (N)

This is the scientific meaning of weight. But it is commonly used in English to mean mass in kg. For example, we say 'He used to weigh 85 kg but since his illness he has lost weight.' This is why the word 'weight' in science is likely to cause misconceptions.

newton: the unit of measure for weight, named after Isaac Newton, who explained the force of gravity

forcemeter: a device to weigh objects in newtons (N)

weightlessness: a state of having no weight because there is no gravity

astronaut: a person who goes into space

rehabilitation: to restore your body to health

In this unit we use the word to describe how astronauts must restore their bodies to health after a period of time spent in space.

In everyday English we talk about people having to rehabilitate after they have had an operation or a long illness.

We also describe animals and plants rehabilitating if their habitat has been destroyed and they are re-growing somewhere else.

Common misconceptions

Misconception	How to identify	How to overcome
Mass and weight mean the same thing and they are equal at all times.	Ask learners if, when they stand on a scale, they are finding out their weight or their mass. See Starter idea 2. If they say both, they have the misconception. If they say 'weight' they are scientifically wrong. Question 3 of 'Getting started' will also elicit the misconception.	This is a completely expected misconception because of the way we use the words 'weight' and 'weigh'. Read through What is the difference between mass and weight? in the Learner's Book.

Starter ideas

1 Getting started (5 minutes)

Learning intention: To revise that the force of gravity keeps the Moon in orbit around the Earth.

To introduce the idea that an astronaut does not weigh the same on the Moon as on Earth

Resources: Learner's Book; Digital Classroom video: Missions to the Moon (optional)

Description: Ask learners what the photograph shows (an astronaut on the Moon).

Then ask questions 1–2 and hopefully learners will know the answers. Otherwise revise this. Then ask question 3 and see what answers they come up with. You will be answering the question in the first part of the topic.

> **Digital Classroom:** If you have access to the Digital Classroom component, show the video 'Missions to the Moon'. The i button will explain how to use the video.

2 How much does it weigh? (5 minutes)

Learning intention: To show that we use the word 'weight' when scientifically we mean mass

Resources: A bathroom or kitchen scale, a book

Description: Ask a learner to put a book on the scale and another learner to read its weight. They will read the weight in kg which is a scientifically incorrect use of the word 'weight' (explain that it should be mass).

Main teaching ideas

1 Activity 1: What is the difference between mass and weight? (30 minutes)

Learning intention: Describe the difference between mass measured in kilograms (kg) and weight measured in newtons (N).

Resources: Learner's Book

Description: Look at the picture of the baby being weighed and read the first paragraph. This explains that we misuse the words 'weigh' and 'weight' when we should, scientifically, be saying 'mass'.

Then read the explanation about weight. This concept is NOT an easy one and you may find many learners take a while to get the hang of it.

Go through the explanation at least twice.

Then let learners work alone or in pairs to write down the answers to questions 1–3 in their notebooks. They can discuss the answer to question 4 and then report back.

> **Differentiation ideas:** Questions 1 and 2 are straightforward and questions 3 and 4 are more challenging.

> **Assessment ideas:** Ask learners to take turns to give you their answers. Each time someone gives an answer, ask the class whether they think the answer is correct. If not, ask what they think the answer is. This way you will get a selection of answers and be able to tell them which ones are correct.

2 Think like a scientist: Measure the mass and weight of objects (1 hour including answering the questions and feedback)

Learning intention: To measure the mass and weight of objects.

To record measurements in a table.

To describe a pattern in results and identify if results do not fit the pattern.

To decide when it is necessary to repeat these measurements to give more reliable data.

To make a conclusion from results using scientific knowledge.

Resources: Learner's Book

Each group will need: a scale to measure mass, a forcemeter to measure weight, a plastic carrier bag, objects of different masses to measure, such as different vegetables or fruits, packets of rice or sugar, pencil cases and books

Description: All learners should draw the table in their notebooks. They can copy the results from the learner who did the recording during the activity.

Follow the instructions in the Learner's Book.

When they have finished clearing up, all learners should answer the questions in their notebooks.

> **Practical guidance:** You could assign these tasks to groups of six learners:

- Learner 1: enters the results in the table.
- Learner 2: keeps time. Their job is to monitor progress and keep the group within the time frame you have given them.
- Learner 3: puts the object in the carrier bag and on the scale.
- Learner 4: reads the mass in kilograms and gives result to Learner 1.
- Learner 5: keeps the object in the carrier bag and puts it on the hook of the forcemeter.
- Learner 6: reads the weight in newtons and gives result to Learner 1.
- All learners combine efforts to tidy up when finished.

> **Differentiation ideas:** All learners should be able to answer questions 1–3. Question 4 needs clear thinking and explanation.

> **Assessment ideas:** Move around the classroom while learners are working in groups. Answer any questions they may have. Assess how well each group is working together. Make a note of possible changes to roles for the next group activity.

Have a feedback session where you go through answers to the questions. Pay particular attention to learners' answers to question 4. Correct if necessary.

3 Activity 2: How gravity affects weight in space (30 minutes)

Learning intention: Describe the effect of gravity and know that when gravity changes, the weight of an object changes but the mass does not.

Resources: Learner's Book

More pictures of astronauts in space and the International Space Station

Description: Read the Weightlessness text in the Learner's Book to the learners. This is a very good section to address the Science in Context objective: 6SIC.04 Identify people who use science, including professionally, in their area and describe how they use science.

Show them pictures of the International Space Station and astronauts in space.

Get learners to imagine what it is like to be floating and have everything around you floating. How do you drink a glass of water? How do you clean your teeth?

Learners can then answer the questions in Activity 2 in pairs. They can discuss their thoughts about the answer to question 9.

> **Differentiation ideas:** This will hopefully appeal to learners and they will be able to see how gravity affects weight. Questions 7 and 8 address this. All the answers except for question 9 are in the text so all learners will be able to answer the questions. If they are not sure of an answer, show them the sentence in the text that has the answer. Maybe they do not understand some of the words so you can explain them again.

> **Assessment ideas:** Learners can share their answers in class.

Plenary ideas

1 Weight or mass (5 minutes)

Resources: Give pairs of learners two cards – one saying WEIGHT and the other MASS.

Description: Learners must hold up the correct card to answer questions.

Ask learners questions such as:

What is measured in newtons? (Weight)

What is measured with a forcemeter? (Weight)

Tom weighs 52 kg – is this his weight or mass? (Mass)

On the Moon, will Tom's weight or mass stay the same? (Mass)

What is measured in kilograms? (Mass)

Which of these is dependent on the force of gravity? (Weight)

› **Assessment ideas:** Check the cards to make sure they are getting the correct answers.

› **Reflection ideas:** See Learner's Book: Did the practical activity help you to understand the difference between mass and weight?

2 **Focus or Practice (10 minutes)**

Resources: Workbook

Description: Learners answer questions in the Workbook. They can choose which of the two activities to do according to their confidence level.

› **Assessment ideas:** Pair up with a learner who has chosen the same activity and mark each other's work.

CROSS-CURRICULAR LINKS

Reading scales accurately and converting kilograms to newtons (and vice versa) is linked with Mathematics.

Homework idea 3 is linked with English – new vocabulary, sentence construction and creative writing.

Homework ideas

1 Learners could work through the Workbook Focus, Practice and/or Challenge. The Focus exercise is a simple consolidation activity.

The Practice exercise offers practice in entering results in a table.

The Challenge activity requires learners to read a forcemeter, calculate mass and calculate weight on the Moon.

2 Learners could complete Worksheets 5.1A, B or C – see below.

3 Imagine you are an astronaut. Write a story about a day in your life in space. You can include pictures. Bring your story to class and read it to the class.

Topic Worksheets

Worksheet 5.1: Case study: Isaac Newton

These three differentiated worksheets are accompanied by a case study about Isaac Newton. Each learner should get a copy of the case study.

Worksheet 5.1A helps learners who are struggling with English to understand the vocabulary in the case study and answer simple questions.

In Worksheet 5.1B, learners have to write their own sentences.

In Worksheet 5.1C, learners answer more complex questions and do some research.

5.2 The effects of forces

LEARNING PLAN

Learning objectives	Learning intention	Success criteria
6Pf.03 Use force diagrams to show the name, size and direction of forces acting on an object.	• Use force diagrams to show the name, size and direction of forces acting on an object.	• Learners can use force diagrams to describe effects of forces.

CONTINUED

Learning objectives	Learning intention	Success criteria
6Pf.04 Describe the effect of different forces on an object at rest and in motion.	• Describe the effect of different forces on an object at rest and in motion.	• Learners can investigate the effect of different forces on an object at rest and in motion.
6TWSp.02 Know the features of the five main types of scientific enquiry.	• Practise observing over time.	• Learners can observe the effects of forces on a ball at rest and moving.
6TWSm.02 Use models, including diagrams, to represent and describe scientific phenomena and ideas.	• Use force diagrams to show the name, size and direction of forces acting on an object.	• Learners can use force diagrams to describe effects of forces.

Common misconceptions

Misconception	How to identify	How to overcome
If an object is stationary it has no forces acting on it.	Ask questions 1 and 2 in Getting started. If a learner answers 'the ball is at rest and there are no forces acting on it', they have the misconception.	Do question 3 in the Getting started activity – this shows gravity and normal forces acting on a ball at rest.

Starter ideas

1 Wind is blowing (5 minutes)

Learning intention: To talk about the effect of wind blowing on objects.

Description: Ask learners to think about being outside on a windy day. How does the wind affect the trees?

(The force of the wind makes things move – branches bend, leaves, flowers or seeds blow off.)

How does the force of the wind blowing affect you?

(Hair moves in wind, hat blows off.)

2 Getting started (10 minutes)

Learning intention: To revise what they know about forces on an object at rest.

Resources: Learner's Book

Description: Learners could answer the questions in their notebooks or you could project the picture on to the whiteboard and get learners to come up to the board and draw on the force arrows. Ask the class whether they are correct or not.

Main teaching ideas

1 Think like a scientist: Investigate the effects of different forces on an object (40 minutes)

Learning intention Describe the effect of different forces on an object at rest and in motion.

Resources: Learner's Book

Each group needs: a ping-pong ball, a straw, a table, a book, a table cloth or towel

Do the investigation on a flat table top or on the floor

Description: Follow the instructions 1–6 in the Learner's Book. Each action creates a force on the ball. Learners discuss in their group the effects of the different forces on the ball.

> **Practical guidance:** Learners can work in small groups of 3–5. Each learner can have a turn doing the actions.

> **Differentiation ideas:** This investigation is suitable for all abilities.

> **Assessment ideas:** Walk around the class while groups are busy doing the investigation. Help where necessary. Take note of how learners behave in the group situation. Ask groups if each learner is getting a chance to do the actions. Are some learners not participating?

2 Activity 1: The effects of forces (40 minutes including feedback)

Learning intentions: Use force diagrams to show the name, size and direction of forces acting on an object.

Describe the effect of different forces on an object at rest and in motion.

Resources: Learner's Book; Digital Classroom activity: Effects of forces (optional)

Description: It is important that learners do this activity as soon as possible after they have finished the investigation with the ping-pong ball, when it is fresh in their minds. Learners must write and draw their answers in their notebooks.

> **Digital Classroom:** If you have access to the Digital Classroom component, use the activity 'Effects of forces' to check learners understanding of this topic. The i button will explain how to use the activity.

> **Differentiation ideas:** The activity should be suitable for all learners.

> **Assessment ideas:** Go through answers when learners have finished. Ask a learner to come and draw their force diagrams on the board. Ask learners if they have the same drawings or if theirs are different in order to identify whether learners have made mistakes; and if they have, make sure they understand where they went wrong.

3 Activity 2: Identify the effects of forces in ball games (10 minutes)

Learning intention: Describe the effect of different forces on an object at rest and in motion.

Resources: Learner's Book

Description: Identify the games the children are playing in the pictures (baseball or rounders, soccer, snooker, cricket).

Talk about what forces the children are applying to the balls (catching, kicking, pushing, hitting).

Let learners identify the effects of these forces by answering the questions. They can work in pairs.

> **Practical guidance:** Question 5 involves playing a ball game and thinking about what forces they apply to the ball and what effects these forces have

on the ball. Ask learners what ball games they can play and give them some suggestions – it can be a really simple game such as throwing a ball to each other or bouncing a ball off a wall.

> **Differentiation ideas:** This activity is suitable for all learners. Go around the class to find out what ball game they played. Some learners who may have struggled with the more formal parts of the activity may well understand better by actually playing a ball game.

> **Assessment ideas:** Compare answers from different pairs.

Plenary ideas

1 The effects of forces in sport (10 minutes)

Description: Ask learners to tell you what sports they like to play or watch on TV.

Write the names of the sports on the board.

For each sport, ask learners what forces are involved in the sport – e.g. kicking a football, throwing a netball, hitting a cricket ball, catching a ball.

Then ask learners what effects these forces have, e.g. the ball moves, it changes direction, it stops, it slows down, etc.

> **Assessment ideas:** Some learners will be more vocal than others. Encourage all learners to participate so that you can get an idea of how much the whole class knows.

> **Reflection ideas:** See the Learner's Book.

2 The wind creates different forces on the tree (10 minutes)

Description: Return to Starter idea 1. Ask learners:

What is the effect on the tree when it is windy? (Branches bend and sway, leaves fall to the ground.)

When do the leaves stop moving? (When they reach the ground.)

When the leaves reach the ground, do they move along the ground as fast as they moved through the air? (No, the ground offers more friction force and the leaves do not move so fast.)

Does the force of the wind cause the leaves to change their shape? (If the leaves are dry they break up.)

> **Assessment ideas:** Encourage the quieter learners to give answers.

> **Reflection ideas:** See the Learner's Book.

Homework ideas

1 Learners could complete the Focus activity in the Workbook. The Focus activity is suitable for learners who are not very confident. Learners have to match four different effects of forces to four drawings supplied.

2 Learners could then complete the Practice activity in the Workbook. It is more demanding because learners must think up the effects of forces illustrated on drawings. They also have to draw a force diagram.

Alternatively, learners could go on to work through the Challenge activity in the Workbook. In the Challenge activity, learners must demonstrate five different effects of forces using the given resources and present their answers in a table.

3 Research pottery: people who make objects out of clay exert force on the clay. Describe what changes happen to the clay. Find some pictures to illustrate these changes.

Answers

Forces on clay change its shape. For example, you can press clay into a flat shape or roll clay into a sausage shape or roll it into a ball.

5.3 Floating and sinking

LEARNING PLAN

Learning objectives	Learning intention	Success criteria
6Pf.05 Recognise that the mass and shape of an object can affect if it floats or sinks.	• Find out that the mass and shape of an object can affect if it floats or sinks.	• Learners can find out that the mass and shape of an object can affect if it floats or sinks.
6Pf.03 Use force diagrams to show the name, size and direction of forces acting on an object.	• Use force diagrams to describe effects of forces.	• Learners can use force diagrams to describe effects of forces.
6TWSp.02 Know the features of the five main types of scientific enquiry.	• Practise fair testing and pattern seeking.	• Learners can do scientific enquiries involving fair testing and pattern seeking.
6TWSp.03 Make predictions, referring to relevant scientific knowledge and understanding within familiar and unfamiliar contexts.	• Make predictions, and find out whether our predictions were correct.	• Learners can make predictions, and find out whether our predictions were correct.
6TWSc.05 Take appropriately accurate measurements.	• Take accurate measurements.	• Learners can take accurate measurements.
6TWSa.02 Describe patterns in results, including identifying any anomalous results.	• Describe patterns in results, and identify any results that do not fit the pattern.	• Learners can describe a pattern in results and identify any results that do not fit the pattern.

CONTINUED

Learning objectives	Learning intention	Success criteria
6TWSa.01 Describe the accuracy of predictions, based on results.	• Make predictions, and find out whether our predictions were correct.	• Learners can make predictions, and find out whether our predictions were correct.
6TWSa.03 Make a conclusion from results informed by scientific understanding.	• Make a conclusion from results using science knowledge about floating and sinking.	• Learners can make a conclusion from results using science knowledge about floating and sinking.
6TWSa.05 Present and interpret results using tables, bar charts, dot plots, line graphs and scatter graphs.	• Collect and record observations and measurements in tables. • Present results in a scatter graph.	• Learners can collect and record observations and measurements in tables. • Learners can present results in a scatter graph.
6TWSm.02 Use models, including diagrams, to represent and describe scientific phenomena and ideas.	• Use force diagrams to describe effects of forces.	• Learners can use force diagrams to describe effects of forces.

LANGUAGE SUPPORT

The key terms for this topic are:

upthrust: a force that pushes up to an object in water or air

displaced: the moving aside of water as a result of upthrust. For example, a boat pushes water aside or displaces the same mass of water as the mass of the boat.

In everyday English we use the word 'displaced' when something or somebody has lost their home.

Additionally, you may want to revise the following two words which learners came across at an earlier stage:

float: an object will float when its mass is equal to or less than the mass of water displaced by upthrust

In everyday English, we have clouds floating in the sky.

sink: to fall downwards slowly. An object will sink when its mass is more than the mass of water displaced by upthrust.

In everyday English we use the noun 'sink' to describe the bowl in the kitchen where you do the washing up.

Common misconceptions

Misconception	How to identify	How to overcome
Heavy objects sink and light objects float, regardless of their size or shape.	In the Getting started activity, if learners say the coin sinks because it is heavy and the cork floats because it is light.	Later in the topic learners will see that the coin sinks because it has a greater mass than the mass of water it displaces when put on the water.

Starter ideas

1 Getting started (10 minutes)

Learning intention: To find out what learners know about sinking and floating

Resources: Learner's Book

A glass bowl of water, a cork and a coin

Description: Ask the questions in class and demonstrate with the cork and coin.

2 Does the orange float? (10 minutes)

Learning intention: To find out if learners have misconceptions about floating and sinking.

Resources: A bowl of water and 2 oranges – one with skin on and the other peeled

Description: Ask learners whether they think the whole orange will sink or float (they will probably say sink). It floats!

Ask learners whether they think the peeled orange will sink or float (they will probably say float). It sinks! Even though it has to be lighter than when the skin was on!

(The peel contains a lot of air and causes the mass per unit volume to be less than the unpeeled orange, which helps the orange to float.)

Main teaching ideas

1 Forces acting on objects when they float or sink (1 hour)

Learning intentions: To find out that the mass of an object can affect if it floats or sinks.

To use force diagrams to describe effects of forces.

To make predictions and find out whether our predictions were correct.

To plan a fair test and identify the independent, dependent and control variables.

To take accurate measurements.

To collect and record observations and measurements in tables.

Resources: Learner's Book; Digital Classroom video: Archimedes and displacement (optional)

For each group: a large plastic container half-full of water, a measuring scale, a small plastic container, sand (or flour or rice), a spoon

Description: Begin by reading through the section in the Learner's Book under the heading Forces acting on objects when they float or sink.

› **Digital Classroom:** If you have access to the Digital Classroom component, show the video 'Archimedes and displacement'. The i button will explain how to use the video.

The key concept here is the force diagram showing floating and sinking. However, this is a half way point in understanding the concept fully (see Background knowledge) since in Stage 7 learners will find out that density (mass per unit volume) is the clearest explanation (it explains the orange example better).

Some learners may query why we are talking about mass when gravity is measuring weight. This is a good point! But tell them we are not comparing floating and sinking on the Earth and the Moon, so we can use mass.

Next, get all learners to do Think like a scientist 1: How does mass affect floating and sinking?

All learners should begin by making a results table as described in Step 1. Tell learners to think in their groups about the control, dependent and independent variables when they do the activity.

› **Practical guidance:** Learners should work in groups of 4–6.

Give them a time limit – 30 minutes should be enough. Tell them how much time they have left at regular intervals.

Learners can take turns to measure and to carefully place a container on the water.

› **Differentiation ideas:** The activity is straightforward in that all learners should be able to see clearly how mass affects whether an object floats or sinks. However, you may have some questions from learners to answer. For example, some learners may be confused by our everyday use of the word 'weight' and 'weigh' when it is scientifically correct to say 'mass'. Also, they may be confused by the fact that the diagrams show the force of gravity pushing objects down and they have learnt in the previous topic that this is weight not mass. But remind them that we are not comparing whether our container floats or sinks here on Earth with what happens on another planet where the gravity is different. We could measure the weight of the sand or rice in newtons but remember this would just be ten-times the mass, so the comparisons would be the same.

› **Assessment ideas:** Walk around the class while learners are doing the activity. Note how groups are working together and whether they are improving their group work skills.

2 Activity: Fair testing, force diagrams and writing a conclusion (20 minutes)

Learning intentions: To find out that the mass of an object can affect if it floats or sinks.

To use force diagrams to describe the effects of forces.

To practise fair testing and identify the independent, dependent and control variables.

To make a conclusion from results informed by scientific understanding.

Resources: Learner's Book

Description: Following the Think like a scientist activity in Main teaching idea 1; learners answer questions in their notebooks

> **Assessment ideas:** It is important that you go through their answers before starting the next section.

Learners could compare answers within their group and then as a class. Get learners to draw their force diagrams on the board. If some learners have made mistakes, make sure they understand where they went wrong.

3 Think like a scientist 2: How does shape affect floating and sinking? (60 minutes)

Learning intentions: To find out that the shape of an object can affect if it floats or sinks.

To make predictions and find out whether our predictions were correct.

To practise fair testing and pattern seeking.

To plan a fair test and identify the independent, dependent and control variables.

To suggest how to change the shape of a boat to carry more mass and still float.

To make a conclusion from results informed by scientific understanding.

To present results in a scatter graph.

Resources: Learner's Book

Each group needs: a large container half-full of water, 10 marbles, aluminium foil dish, aluminium foil (bring a roll of heavy aluminium foil and groups can tear off what they need)

Description: Follow the instructions in the Learner's Book.

For Step 4, learners can all help with the design and can try different shapes from the same piece of aluminium foil and test each one.

This section links with 6SIC.04 Identify people who use science, including professionally, in their area and describe how they use science.

> **Practical guidance:** Divide class into groups of 4–6 learners. These can be the same groups as earlier or you can swap learners around.

Give them a time limit – 30 minutes should be enough time. Tell them how much time they have left at regular intervals.

After they have finished and cleared up they must all write answers to the questions in their notebooks. You may like to give them question 6 to do for Homework.

> **Differentiation ideas:** Suitable for all learners. You may still have some questions from learners to answer regarding the mass/weight issue – see above in Main teaching idea 2 for suggestions on how to deal with these.

Question 4 will encourage learners who have a flair for design.

Question 5 is more challenging.

Question 6 gives learners the opportunity to use data to draw a scatter graph. Some learners may have forgotten how to draw a scatter graph or find it difficult – direct them to the instructions on how to draw a scatter graph in the New science skills section at the end of the Learner's Book.

> **Assessment ideas:** Learners can all share their boat designs at the end of the lesson

4 Other ways to make objects float (10 minutes)

Learning intention: To find out that the mass and shape of an object can affect if it floats or sinks.

Resources: Images of objects floating that contain air, such as:

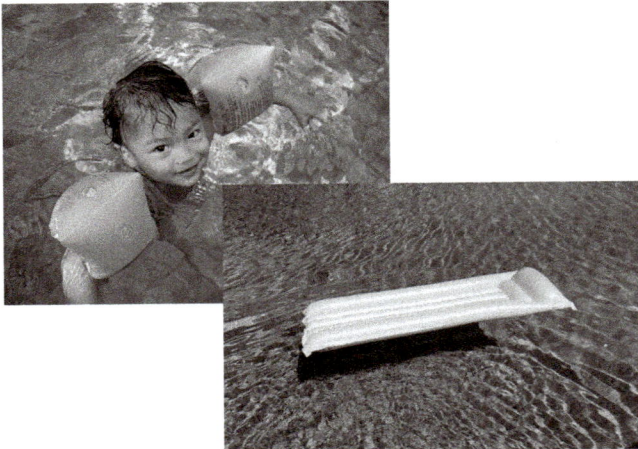

Description: This activity does not appear in the Learner's Book.

Show learners the example images of swimming armbands and a lilo, or similar ones you have found yourself. Explain that objects which are light for their size often float. An object can be light for its size if it contains air, such as a hollow ball or the cork you used at the start of the topic. The hollow sections increase the size of the object and the upthrust for very little increase in the downwards force of gravity.

Get learners to work in groups to think of other examples. If you think they need some hints tell them to think of packaging materials.

Answers

Polystyrene is a material that contains lots of air and floats. It is used for packaging.

Surf boards are made of polystyrene so they can float on the sea.

Boats that are too heavy have polystyrene pumped into containers to make them float.

Life jackets and life belts contain polystyrene.

⟩ **Differentiation ideas:** This activity is suitable for all learners.

⟩ **Assessment ideas:** Learners can all share their ideas in class

Plenary ideas

1 Boat designs (10 minutes)

Resources: Aluminium boats

Description: Hold up each group's aluminium boat from Think like a scientist 2: How does shape affect floating and sinking?

Find out which group's boat held the most marbles before it sank. Get learners to discuss the design features that allowed the boat to carry more or, in some cases, fewer marbles.

⟩ **Assessment ideas:** Encourage as much participation as possible.

⟩ **Reflection ideas:** Ask learners, next time they see a boat (a canoe, a rowing boat, a yacht or a cruise liner), to think about how the design of the boat keeps it floating.

2 Focus (10 minutes)

Resources: Workbook

Description: Learners answer questions in the Workbook

⟩ **Assessment ideas:** If you have time at the end of the lesson, go through the answers and learners can check their own work. Otherwise you can do this at the start of your next lesson.

Homework ideas

1 Learners could answer question 6 in the set of questions after How does shape affect floating and sinking? This will give learners practice in drawing a scatter graph.

2 Learners could complete the Focus (if not done during the lesson) activity in the Workbook.

3 They could then go on to work through the Practice and/or Challenge activities in the Workbook.

The Practice activity is based on a similar investigation to the one in the topic. Learners have to answer questions about variables as well as how the shape of an object affects floating and sinking.

The Challenge activity has a short case study about submarines, so it will be more challenging from a language point of view, and also includes some reference work.

5.4 Different circuits and circuit diagrams

LEARNING PLAN

Learning objectives	Learning intention	Success criteria
6Pe.01 Use conventional symbols to draw circuit diagrams and make and compare circuits that include cells, switches, lamps and buzzers.	• Use conventional symbols to draw circuit diagrams. • Make and compare circuits that include batteries, switches and buzzers.	• Learners can use conventional symbols to draw circuit diagrams. • Learners can make and compare circuits that include batteries, switches, lamps and buzzers and represent these with circuit diagrams.
6Pe.02 Make simple circuits and compare the brightness of lamps in series and parallel circuits.	• Compare the brightness of lamps in series and parallel circuits.	• Learners can compare the brightness of lamps in series and parallel circuits.
6TWSp.02 Know the features of the five main types of scientific enquiry.	• Identify and classify circuits as series or parallel.	• Learners can identify and classify circuits as series or parallel.
6TWSp.03 Make predictions, referring to relevant scientific knowledge and understanding within familiar and unfamiliar contexts.	• Make predictions, referring to what you know about electricity and test to see if your predictions are correct.	• Learners can make predictions, referring to what you know about electricity and test to see if your predictions are correct.
6TWSp.05 Describe risks when planning practical work and consider how to minimise them.	• Describe risks when planning practical work and consider how to minimise them.	• Learners can describe risks when planning practical work and consider how to minimise them.
6TWSc.03 Choose equipment to carry out an investigation and use it appropriately.	• Choose components to make circuits.	• Learners can choose components to make circuits.
6TWSc.04 Decide when observations and measurements need to be repeated to give more reliable data.	• Decide when observations need to be repeated to give more reliable results.	• Learners can decide when observations need to be repeated to give more reliable results.
6TWSc.08 Collect and record observations and/or measurements in tables and diagrams appropriate to the type of scientific enquiry.	• Present and interpret results in tables.	• Learners can present and interpret results in tables.
6TWSc.06 Carry out practical work safely.	• Carry out practical work safely.	• Learners can carry out practical work safely.

CONTINUED

Learning objectives	Learning intention	Success criteria
6TWSa.01 Describe the accuracy of predictions, based on results.	• Make predictions, referring to what you know about electricity and test to see if your predictions are correct.	• Learners can make predictions, referring to what you know about electricity and test to see if your predictions are correct.
6TWSa.03 Make a conclusion from results informed by scientific understanding.	• Make a conclusion from results using your understanding of electricity.	• Learners can make a conclusion from results using your understanding of electricity.
6TWSm.02 Use models, including diagrams, to represent and describe scientific phenomena and ideas.	• Use conventional symbols to draw circuit diagrams.	• Learners can use conventional symbols to draw circuit diagrams.

LANGUAGE SUPPORT

The key terms for this topic are:

circuit diagram: a diagram of a circuit using conventional symbols for all the components

symbol: a small sign used on a diagram to represent a real thing. For example, the symbol ✓ means 'correct' and the symbol ✗ means 'wrong'

conventional symbol: a symbol that is recognised all over the world

volt (V): the unit for measuring the strength of electricity

voltage: the strength of electricity needed for an electrical component or appliance to work

series circuit: a circuit where the electric current only has one pathway

parallel circuit: a circuit where there is more than one pathway and each pathway receives the full circuit voltage

Starter ideas

1 Getting started (5 minutes)

Learning intention: To make sure learners remember what they learnt about circuits in Stage 4.

Resources: Learner's Book

Description: Look at the picture of the circuit in the Learner's Book. Ask different learners to answer the questions. Make sure everyone agrees with or corrects their answers.

2 Draw a circuit (5–10 minutes)

Learning intention: To see how long it takes to draw a circuit – this will make circuit diagrams seem a great idea!

Resources: Learner's Book

Description: This activity does not appear in the Learner's Book.

Ask learners to copy the picture of a circuit with the battery, switch and lamp in a lamp holder. Or get volunteers to come and draw it on the board.

Then ask them 'Would you like to learn a quick way to draw a circuit?'

Main teaching ideas

1 Circuit diagrams (40 minutes)

Learning intentions: To use conventional symbols to draw circuit diagrams.

To make and compare circuits that include batteries, switches and buzzers.

Resources: Learner's Book

Description: Read the text under Circuit diagrams. Show them how quickly they can draw the circuit now!

Look carefully at the pictures of components with their symbols.

Tell learners they can keep referring to this page until they can remember the symbols.

Learners can practise using the symbols by answering the questions in Activity: Use circuit symbols to read and draw circuit diagrams.

They should write and draw their answers in their notebooks.

> **Differentiation ideas:** All learners should be able to manage this activity. The questions begin with easy circuits to identify using the reference in the Learner's Book. Then they move on to drawing their own circuits in questions 4 and 5. Some learners will find it difficult to draw the circuit diagrams to begin with. You may be able to help with these suggestions:

Tell learners they may find it easier to begin by drawing a rectangle to represent the connecting wire for the circuit using a ruler and a pencil. Then they can rub out sections with an eraser and draw in their components.

They can keep on referring to the list of components and symbols in the Learner's Book until they can remember them.

Point out the small differences in some of the symbols. For example, two 1.5V cells joined together have a small length of wire between them to show they are joined, whereas a 3V battery does not have this short piece of connecting wire because the battery is one unit.

> **Assessment ideas:** Ask different learners to give you the answers to the questions so that everyone can check their work.

Learners can check their own progress by asking the How am I doing? question in the Learner's Book

2 Think like a scientist 1: Build circuits with different components (60 minutes)

Learning intentions: To use conventional symbols to draw circuit diagrams.

To choose components to make circuits.

To make and compare circuits that include batteries, switches and buzzers.

To make predictions, referring to what you know about electricity and test to see if your predictions are correct.

To describe risks when planning practical work and consider how to minimise them.

To carry out practical work safely.

To decide when observations need to be repeated to give more reliable results.

To make a conclusion from results using your understanding of electricity.

Resources: Each group will need: two 1.5V cells, a 3V battery, a switch, a lamp, a buzzer, connecting wires

Description: Follow the steps for making the circuits in Practical guidance.

When groups have finished and tidied up, they can answer the follow-up questions and draw their circuit diagrams.

> **Practical guidance:** Divide class into groups of 4–6 learners. Each group needs a flat surface to work on.

In their groups learners can discuss Step 1 and come and choose the components they need from you. That way you can check they are using the correct components.

Next they must discuss the risks – cutting away from them if they need to take plastic covering off wires; not touching the bare wires when the circuit is closed.

Before they make each circuit they must predict what will happen when they complete the circuit – will the lamp come on? Will the buzzer make a noise? Will the buzzer sound louder if we add another 1.5V cell to the battery?

Then test their predictions.

If they are not sure they have made a circuit correctly, they should check and repeat to see if they get the same result.

Walk around from group to group offering guidance and advice and encouragement.

> **Differentiation ideas:** Hopefully learners will be getting more confident working in their groups. Encourage group members to help each other.

> **Assessment ideas:** When you go through the answers to the questions it would be a good idea to get a group to come and demonstrate their circuit so that learners can see if they have answered the questions correctly.

Ask for volunteers to draw the circuit diagrams on the board.

3 Think like a scientist 2: Make and compare a series circuit and a parallel circuit (60 minutes)

Learning intentions: To use conventional symbols to draw circuit diagrams.

To identify and classify circuits as series or parallel.

To compare the brightness of lamps in series and parallel circuits.

To make predictions, referring to what you know about electricity and test to see if your predictions are correct.

To describe risks when planning practical work and consider how to minimise them.

To carry out practical work safely.

To make a conclusion from results using your understanding of electricity.

Resources: Learner's Book

Each group will need: plastic coated wire, four lamps in lamp holders, two 3 V batteries

Description: Point out that in all the circuits learners have made so far, the electricity can only take one path. These are called series circuits (because all the components are linked one after the other).

These circuits have a disadvantage because if one lamp or buzzer is faulty, the others in the circuit will not light up or buzz. This is why we use parallel circuits where there is more than one path for the electricity to go. Each lamp or buzzer has its own circuit.

Before learners start to make their circuits they must all prepare a results table as shown in the Learner's Book.

When learners have made and tested their circuits they must clear up and then write answers to the questions and draw their circuit diagrams in their notebooks.

> **Practical guidance:** Divide class into groups of 4–6 learners. Each group needs a flat surface to work on.

Warn learners not to unscrew the lamps when they are hot. They should disconnect for a few minutes until the lamp cools down and then unscrew the lamp.

Before learners make each circuit they must predict what will happen when they complete the circuit – will one lamp shine more brightly than the other or will they shine with equal brightness?

Once they have built their circuits, learners should then test their predictions and record their results in their table. (If they are not sure they have made a circuit correctly, they should check and repeat to see if they get the same result.)

Walk around from group to group offering guidance and advice and encouragement.

> **Differentiation ideas:** Some learners will be better at practical work than others. But all learners will get better with practice. So it is important to encourage learners to work together in their group and learn from each other.

> **Assessment ideas:** See below in Plenary idea 1

Plenary ideas

1 Questions after Think like a scientist 2: Make and compare a series circuit and a parallel circuit (10–20 minutes)

Resources: Learner's Book; Digital Classroom activity: Circuit diagrams (optional)

Description: If necessary give learners more time to finish the questions.

> **Digital Classroom:** If you have access to the Digital Classroom component, use the activity Circuit diagrams to consolidate learners understanding. The i button will explain how to use this activity.

> **Assessment ideas:** Go through learners' answers so that you can be sure that they have all understood the differences between a series and parallel circuit.

Ask different learners to give you the answers to questions 1 and 2 and come and draw their circuit diagrams on the board.

Check that everyone has their conclusion correct.

Get two different learners to give you the answers to question 6.

> **Reflection ideas:** See the Learner's Book question: How did the practical activities help you to understand the differences between series and parallel circuits?

2 Know your circuit symbols (10 minutes)

Resources: Make some cards with different circuit symbols on.

Description: Distribute the cards to the class. Then ask questions such as:

What is the symbol for a lamp?

What is the symbol for a 3 V battery?

Learners with the card with the correct symbol must hold it up.

> **Assessment ideas:** This is a fun way to help learners to remember the symbols.

Homework ideas

1 Learners could complete the Focus activity in the Workbook. This is a good activity for learners to consolidate what they know about circuit symbols.

2 Learners could move onto the Practice activity in the Workbook. This provides practice with drawing circuit diagrams and series and parallel circuits.

Learners could then move onto the Challenge activity in the Workbook. This provides practice on unfamiliar examples.

3 Alternatively, learners could work through Worksheet 5.4 – see details below.

Topic Worksheet

Worksheet 5.4: Planning lamps and switches for a flat

This is a great worksheet for showing learners the practical use of circuit diagrams and understanding series and parallel circuits.

The Help sheet guides learners through the activity step by step.

The Stretch question is where learners really become electricians!

PROJECT GUIDANCE

6SIC.01 Describe how scientific knowledge and understanding changes over time through the use of evidence gained by enquiry.

Tell learners to search on the internet for information about the three different types of battery. They should restrict the information to just what is relevant, namely:

- the advantages of the battery compared to batteries that were invented earlier
- the disadvantages of the battery
- what the batteries are used for.

For example, they will find out that Cadmium is a poisonous metal, so Nickel cadmium batteries are difficult to dispose of. They can store more energy than previous batteries. But if they are not fully used up when you recharge them they do not hold as much energy the next time you use them.

Photographs and pictures of batteries and the devices they are used in will improve their project.

Stress that they should only produce one A4 page.

Assessment rubric

Here are some guidelines for assessment:

How well did the learner...	Very well	Adequately	Not much effort made
find relevant information about each battery?			
write a short answer to each question?			
include pictures and/ or photographs of batteries and devices?			
arrange all their information on an A4 page?			

Display projects on the classroom wall.

> 6 Light and the solar system

Unit plan

Topic	Approx. number of learning hours	Outline of learning content	Resources
6.1 Reflection	3	• Investigate and use diagrams to describe how light changes direction when it reflects off a plane mirror.	**Learner's Book:** Activity: How we see reflected light Think like a scientist 1: Demonstrate how light travels when it reflects Think like a scientist 2: Make and test a periscope **Workbook:** Topic 6.1 ⤓ Worksheets 6.1A, 6.1B and 6.1C **Digital Classroom:** Activity – Reflection
6.2 Refraction	3	• Do simple investigations to demonstrate refraction and apply this to lenses and rainbows.	**Learner's Book:** Think like a scientist 1: Demonstrate how light travels when it refracts Think like a scientist 2: Make and test a convex lens **Workbook:** Topic 6.2 **Digital Classroom:** Video – Prisms
6.3 The solar system	3	• Use models and diagrams to describe the relative position of the planets, the Moon and the Sun and compare their movements. • Observe the phases of the Moon and describe and explain the changes.	**Learner's Book:** Think like a scientist 1: Make a scale model of the solar system Activity 1: The planets Think like a scientist 2: Observe and describe the phases of the Moon Activity 2: Identify phases of the Moon **Workbook:** Topic 6.3 ⤓ Worksheet 6.3 **Digital Classroom:** Video – Planets in the solar system

Across unit resources		
Learner's Book:	**Teacher's Resource:**	**Digital Classroom:**
Project: Using the Moon's cycle to make a calendar	⬇ Language worksheets 1 & 2	End-of-unit quiz
Check your progress quiz	⬇ Diagnostic test	
	⬇ Mid-year test	
	⬇ End-of-year test	
	⬇ End-of-unit test	

BACKGROUND KNOWLEDGE

In Topic 6.1 you continue talking about Reflection of light where you left off in Stage 5.

To understand refraction in Topic 6.2, you have to know that light is a form of electromagnetism – a combination of electric and magnetic energy and that it travels in waves. Learners will only study this in later stages. For now you are just observing the results of refraction, but you may get some questions in class that require a little background knowledge.

Visible light is a form of energy that travels in waves. The Sun gives off vast amounts of energy in the form of heat (infrared) and light.

When light travels through a vacuum, such as through space, it travels at the huge speed of just under 300 000 km/sec. But if it then travels through water its speed falls to 225 000 km/sec, or if through window glass it falls to 195 000 km/sec. When light changes speed, it bends or 'refracts'. Learners will only cover this at a later stage in science.

In Topic 6.3 you return to the solar system. Distances in space are very difficult to imagine. The Sun is about 400 times larger than the Moon, but the Moon and the Sun look about the same size to us. This is because the Sun is so much further away from us. Think like a scientist 1: Make a scale model of the solar system will be an excellent way to give learners some idea of the scale of the solar system.

Everything in the solar system is moving – even the Sun and the rest of the solar system orbits around the centre of the Milky Way galaxy. The Earth is one of eight planets which revolve around the Sun in orbits. Each planet takes a different length of time to make one orbit, so each planet has a different length of 'year'. Each planet turns on an axis. The times taken for each planet to complete a turn are different, so each planet has its own length of 'day'.

Moons also move in orbits around planets. Our Moon takes $29\frac{1}{2}$ days to complete an orbit. Learners will know that the Moon appears as a different shape at different times, but when they observe the Moon over a month they will see how the shape of the lit up Moon changes slowly. You can explain why we see the different shapes or phases with diagrams in the Learner's Book.

TEACHING SKILLS FOCUS

Making lessons learner-centred

The focus of learner-centred education is the learner and not the teacher. So, as a teacher try to:

Get learners actively involved

Learners who sit passively in front of the teacher who talks at them for the whole lesson are not actively participating in a lesson. Learners do not always have to be conducting experiments or presenting topics to be actively involved. They can also be actively involved by asking questions, having discussions, relating their own experiences and so on in class.

Make the learning experience relevant

It is important for learners to understand the relevance of what they are learning about. There are many examples of how you can do this in this unit – but you are the one who will know about the particular relevance in your country or region.

Allow learners to teach other learners

Provide opportunities for learners to help each other. This encourages co-operation, confidence building and interaction skills. Learners often become more motivated and enthusiastic when they have to demonstrate their knowledge and understanding of a topic to their peers.

Be flexible

As a teacher, you need to be flexible enough to meet the needs of your learners. If you teach the same material to different classes you have probably noticed that each class is different – you have to teach each class in slightly different ways. If you adapt your teaching style to suit your learners, you will keep learners interested, have fewer discipline problems and achieve more success.

Try to act on this advice during this unit.

6.1 Reflection

LEARNING PLAN

Learning objectives	Learning intention	Success criteria
6Ps.01 Describe how a ray of light changes direction when it is reflected from a plane mirror.	• Describe how a ray of light changes direction when it is reflected from a plane mirror.	• Learners can describe how a ray of light changes direction when it is reflected from a plane mirror.
6TWSm.02 Use models, including diagrams, to represent and describe scientific phenomena and ideas.	• Use diagrams to show how light reflects from a plane mirror.	• Learners can use diagrams to show how light reflects from a plane mirror.
6TWSc.04 Decide when observations need to be repeated to give more reliable data.	• Decide when observations need to be repeated to give more reliable data.	• Learners can decide when observations need to be repeated to give more reliable data.
6TWSa.02 Describe patterns in results, including identifying any anomalous results.	• Describe a pattern in results.	• Learners can describe a pattern in results.
6TWSa.03 Make a conclusion from results informed by scientific understanding.	• Make a conclusion from results using knowledge of reflection.	• Learners can make a conclusion from results using knowledge of reflection.

LANGUAGE SUPPORT

Learners will use the following key words in the topic:

mirror image: reflection in a mirror. The best way to explain this is for learners to look at themselves in a mirror – they see a mirror image of themselves

plane mirror: a flat mirror rather than a mirror with a curved surface, such as a concave or convex mirror

normal: a line drawn at right angles (90°) to the surface of the mirror. The word 'normal' is used in everyday English to mean 'usual' or 'average'

incident ray: the ray of light that arrives at the mirror

reflected ray: the ray of light that reflects off the mirror

angle: the space between two lines that meet at a surface, measured in degrees. Learners will have come across angles in Maths. In this unit we are talking about the angle between a light ray and a plane mirror.

periscope: a device that uses mirrors for you to see things otherwise out of sight

Common misconceptions

Misconception	How to identify	How to overcome
Some surfaces such as wood do not reflect any light.	Ask question 5 in the Getting started activity. If learners answer 'no' they have the misconception.	Tell learners all materials reflect some light, otherwise we wouldn't see them. Some materials, like dark wood, absorb more light than they reflect.

Starter ideas

1 Getting started (10 minutes)

Resources: Learner's Book

Description: This activity will revise what learners already know about how light travels, ray diagrams and the type of surface that reflects light best.

Learners can answer questions in pairs and then report back. Then you will get a good idea of what they remember from Stage 5.

If learners answer 'no' to question 5 they have the misconception that surfaces such as wood do not reflect any light. Explain using the How to overcome section above.

2 Mirrors (10 minutes)

Resources: A hand-held mirror for each learner if possible

Description: This activity does not appear in the Learner's Book. It will revise what learners already know about mirrors and how light travels.

Ask learners to look in the mirror and tell you what they see – (themselves, an image).

Ask them why they think the mirror reflects well (smooth, flat shiny surface).

Main teaching ideas

1 Activity: How we see reflected light (30 minutes)

Learning intention: To describe how a ray of light changes direction when it is reflected from a plane mirror.

To use diagrams to show how light reflects from a plane mirror.

Resources: Learner's Book

A lens, a hand mirror, a tennis ball

Description: Read the section under the heading 'Reflected light'. Hold up the mirror as an example of a plane mirror.

Show learners the lens. Point out the curved surface. This is how a lens is different to a plane mirror. They will see later in the topic that it reflects light differently.

Introduce the term 'mirror image'. Discuss the reflection of the flamingo in the lake. Point out that the water must be clear and still for it to act like a mirror.

Move on to 'How does light travel when it reflects?' Get pairs of learners to bounce a tennis ball, like Marcus in the picture, so that they can see that the ball bounces off the ground at the same angle as it arrived.

Point out the incident ray (we called it the arriving ray in Stage 5) and the reflected ray and the normal.

Learners need to consolidate this information, so let them do the Activity in their notebooks before you carry on.

> **Differentiation ideas:** Suitable for all learners.

> **Assessment ideas:** Ask learners to call out answers and come up to the board and draw the answer to question 4. Check that everyone got the correct answers. If not, go through the relevant section again.

2 **Think like a scientist 1: Demonstrate how light travels when it reflects (60 minutes)**

Learning intention: Describe how a ray of light changes direction when it is reflected from a plane mirror.

Use diagrams to show how light reflects from a plane mirror.

Decide when observations need to be repeated to give more reliable data.

Describe a pattern in results.

Make a conclusion from results using knowledge of reflection.

Resources: Learner's Book

For each group: a powerful flashlight, a plane mirror, a sheet of white paper or card about 60 × 60 cm, a piece of black plastic or black paper (enough to cover the flashlight), a pin, masking tape

Description: Ask learners to follow the instructions to shine the ray from the flashlight on to the mirror and observe the angle of incidence and angle of reflection many times – until they have all seen the pattern of angles of incidence and reflection being the same.

Then when learners have cleared away, get them to answer the questions in their notebooks.

> **Practical guidance:** Divide the class into groups. The size of group will depend on how many resources you have. The mirror has to be at least 20 × 20 cm. If you only have one mirror you can do a demonstration, but make sure you get different learners to help and take turns in shining the flashlight on to the mirror.

You will need a darkened room to do this demonstration.

It is better if you can secure the mirror to the wall. If the mirror has hooks you can use these. Otherwise you can tape it to the wall. Make sure it doesn't fall!

Follow the instructions in the Learner's Book.

> **Differentiation ideas:** Some learners will see the pattern straight away, others may take longer. Encourage learners to share ideas within their group and point out the pattern.

> **Assessment ideas:** Get a person from each group to come to the front of the class and give the answers. If there are any differences between the findings of groups, discuss in class to resolve them. Correct where necessary.

3 **Think like a scientist 2: Make and test a periscope (60 minutes)**

Learning intention: Describe how a ray of light changes direction when it is reflected from a plane mirror.

Use diagrams to show how light reflects from a plane mirror.

Decide when observations need to be repeated to give more reliable data.

Describe a pattern in results.

Make a conclusion from results using knowledge of reflection.

Suggest improvements to the design of a periscope.

Resources: Learner's Book

A tall box or carton; 2 small, square plane mirrors, a pencil, a ruler, a protractor to measure the angles, scissors, tape. Digital Classroom activity: Reflection (optional)

Description: Talk about the photograph in the Learner's Book of all the people in the crowd looking through periscopes. Tell learners that people have used the science of how light reflects off mirrors to design periscopes. (This is a way of addressing Learning objective 6SIC.04 Identify people who use science, including professionally, in their area and describe how they use science.)

> **Digital Classroom:** If you have access to the Digital Classroom component, use the activity 'Reflection' to revise what has been learnt about reflection. The i button will explain how to use the activity.

Groups then follow the instructions in the Learner's Book to make periscopes and test them.

Each learner must answer the questions in their notebook (this will take about 15–20 minutes).

> **Practical guidance:** Divide the class into groups of six (or more if you have not got enough mirrors). The mirrors must be able to slide into the slit in the box with a short piece each end sticking out to keep them in place.

Tell groups to do Step 1. Walk around the class to check on groups. Tell them not to make the cuts in the carton until you have checked they have measured their angles correctly.

Once you have checked, they can move on to Steps 2, 3 and 4. Check again before they continue with Steps 5 and 6.

Give them time to have fun testing their periscope. For example, the learner holding the periscope can kneel on the floor with the periscope above the table or desk and see things on the desk. Or a learner could position themselves below a window with the periscope above the window so that they could see outside.

> **Differentiation ideas:** Some learners may find questions 3 and 4 more challenging. As you walk around, check how learners are drawing the periscope. Tell them they only need to do a two-dimensional drawing. If necessary start them off by drawing part of it on the board.

> **Assessment ideas:** Learners should answer the How are we doing? questions to assess how well their group worked.

Plenary ideas

1 Discussion of answers to questions in Think like a scientist 2: Make and test a periscope (10–15 minutes)

Resources: Learner's Book and learners' notebooks

Description: The discussion of answers to these questions will sum up what learners have learnt in this topic.

> **Assessment ideas:** Question 1 has a straightforward answer.

For question 2, you can collect together all the ways the different groups tested their periscopes.

For question 3, get learners to come and draw their periscopes on the board. Make sure the mirrors are facing the correct ways. Explain how the first reflected ray becomes the incident ray for the second mirror. Make sure the angles the incident and reflected rays make with the normal are the same (45°). This will help them to answer question 4.

Question 5 will be a good way to make sure learners understand how a periscope works by applying their knowledge to a different example.

Learners may have different suggestions for the answer to question 6. The obvious answer is to make the periscope taller. Some may also suggest making the frame more sturdy by using a plastic container, for example.

Collect different answers for question 7.

> **Reflection ideas:** Learners can answer the Reflection questions at the end of the topic.

2 Workbook 6.1: Focus exercise (10 minutes)

Resources: Workbook

Description: Learners write and draw answers in the Workbook.

> **Assessment ideas:** Learners can compare their answers with a partner. If they have different answers they can ask you to decide who is correct.

CROSS-CURRICULAR LINKS

The measuring angles tasks are linked to Mathematics.

Homework ideas

1 Workbook 6.1: Practice exercise – this is a good revision activity for the topic where learners have to draw and label diagrams.

2 Workbook 6.1: Challenge exercise – this is an interesting activity on periscopes with information on how they are used in submarines.

3 Learners could complete Worksheet 6.1A, 6.1B or 6.1C – see below for details.

Topic Worksheet

Worksheet 6.1: Optical fibres

Each worksheet is based on some text about optical fibres and how they are used in telecommunications and surgery. Each learner will need a copy of the first page of the Worksheet pack for this topic as well as either Worksheet 6.1A, 6.1B or 6.1C to work through.

For Worksheets 6.1A and 6.1B, learners will need an empty plastic drinks bottle, aluminium foil, sticky tape, a strong flashlight and water.

The three worksheets are differentiated as follows:

Worksheet 6.1A has 'fill in the gaps' answers to questions followed by directions to make a simple model of an optical fibre using a plastic bottle and a flashlight.

Worksheet 6.1B requires learners to answer questions in full sentences. These questions are followed by the directions to make a simple model of an optical fibre using a plastic bottle and a flashlight.

Worksheet 6.1C has questions which need further research on the internet to find the answers.

6.2 Refraction

LEARNING PLAN

Learning objectives	Learning intention	Success criteria
6Ps.02 Describe how a ray of light changes direction when it travels through different mediums and know that this is called refraction.	• Describe how a ray of light changes direction when it travels through different mediums and know that this is called refraction.	• Learners can describe how a ray of light changes direction when it travels through different mediums and know that this is called refraction.
6TWSm.02 Use models, including diagrams, to represent and describe scientific phenomena and ideas.	• Use diagrams to show how light refracts.	• Learners can use diagrams to show how light refracts.
6TWSp.01 Ask scientific questions and select appropriate scientific enquiries to use.	• Ask scientific questions and select appropriate scientific enquiries to use.	• Learners can ask scientific questions and select appropriate scientific enquiries to use.
6TWSp.03 Make predictions, referring to relevant scientific knowledge and understanding within familiar and unfamiliar contexts.	• Make predictions and see if predictions were correct.	• Learners can make predictions and see if predictions were correct.
6TWSa.01 Describe the accuracy of predictions, based on results.	• Make predictions and see if predictions were correct.	• Learners can make predictions and see if predictions were correct.
6TWSa.03 Make a conclusion from results informed by scientific understanding.	• Make a conclusion from results using knowledge of refraction.	• Learners can make a conclusion from results using knowledge of refraction.

LANGUAGE SUPPORT

Learners will use the following key words in the topic:

refract/refraction: the bending of light. For example, light refracts when it moves from water to air

medium: a material such as air, water or glass

This word has several other meanings in English. It is an adjective to describe something in between high and low, or food cooked in between well done and raw.

It is also used to describe the type of work a musician or an artist uses – e.g. the artist uses oils as a medium or the musician plays jazz medium.

A popular use of the word is 'mass media' (media is one of the plurals of medium) – which refers to means of communication such as newspapers, TV and the internet.

optical illusion: something our eyes see but it is not real. The word 'optical' means seen by eyes. An illusion is something that appears but is not real

lens: a transparent material such as glass, Perspex or plastic with at least one curved surface

convex: a bulging shape

converge: to meet or come together

focal point: the point where rays of light converge

Starter ideas

1 Getting started (5 minutes)

Resources: Learner's Book, a glass of water and a white card with two arrows drawn on it as shown in the Learner's Book.

Description: This is a good activity to grab learners' attention and make them want to find out why the arrows changed direction.

Show learners the card with the arrows drawn on it and the glass of water (make sure it is a curved glass like the one in the picture in the Learner's Book).

Tell learners to look carefully at the glass of water. Lower the card.

What has happened to the arrows behind the water? They have changed direction!

Hold the card up away from the glass and the arrows are how they were before! So the arrows only *appear* to turn round.

Is this a magic trick? Ask them if they have an idea as to how the arrows appear to turn around.

2 Lenses (5 minutes)

Resources: A pair of reading glasses

Description: Ask learners who wears eyeglasses (spectacles) for reading to show their eyeglasses to the other learners. Point out the bulging glass. Ask learners how the eyeglasses make it easier for them to read (the lenses make the print larger). Then ask learners how they think the lenses work.

Main teaching ideas

1 Think like a scientist 1: Demonstrate how light travels when it refracts (60 minutes)

Learning intention: Describe how a ray of light changes direction when it travels through different mediums and know that this is called refraction.

Use diagrams to show how light refracts.

Make predictions.

See if predictions were correct.

Make a conclusion from results using knowledge of refraction.

Resources: Learner's Book

A glass of water and pencil for each group, card with arrows on it from the Getting started activity, Digital Classroom video: Prisms (optional)

Description: Before learners tackle this activity, read through the first section under the heading Refraction. This will introduce learners to the new vocabulary: refraction, medium and optical illusion.

Focus on the picture of Sofia looking at the fish. Notice how her eyes think she sees the fish in her direct line of vision. Her eyes don't compensate for the refraction of the light rays. This is why we call it an optical illusion – she thinks she sees something that is not really there.

As soon as they have completed the activity, learners should answer questions 1–7 in their notebooks.

Have a class discussion about the answer to question 8.

> **Practical guidance:** It is absolutely essential that learners do the Think like a scientist activities in this topic themselves. This is a good opportunity for them to practise some of the TWS objectives. You only have to provide a glass of water and a pencil for each group, so it is definitely an activity everyone will be able to participate in.

Divide class into pairs or small groups for the activity.

Tell learners to follow the instructions 1–4 in the Learner's Book. It is important that they predict first, then observe and then look at the pencil to see whether it really has bent!

It is important that learners answer the questions in their notebooks straight away after finishing the activity, before they clear away the glasses and pencils because they have to draw what they see.

> **Digital Classroom:** If you have access to the Digital Classroom component, you could show the video 'Prisms' here. The i button will explain how to use the video.

> **Differentiation ideas:** This is suitable for all learners.

> **Assessment ideas:** Ask learners to answer the 'How are we doing?' questions in the Learner's Book.

Ask different groups to share their answers with the class.

2 Think like a scientist 2: Make and test a convex lens (40 minutes)

Learning intention: Describe how a ray of light changes direction when it travels through different mediums and know that this is called refraction.

Use diagrams to show how light refracts.

Ask scientific questions and select appropriate scientific enquiries to use.

Resources: A convex lens and/or eyeglasses (spectacles), binoculars, telescope to show the class a convex lens

Newspaper or an old magazine, plastic wrap, eye droppers or very small spoons, water

Description: Before learners tackle the activity, show the class a convex lens so that they can see it has a bulge in it. Look at the diagram in the Learner's Book to see how a convex lens causes the light rays to converge at a focal point.

Tell learners that this is how the lenses in our eyes work. If we can't see to read very well we can get eyeglasses with convex lenses to make the print larger for us to read.

Ask learners who wear eyeglasses to show the lenses to the class. Look at the pictures of other things we use that have convex lenses (or at the actual things if you have some in class) – telescope, binoculars, magnifying glass and microscope – all of these things make objects look bigger.

This is a good example of Science in Context 6SIC.04 Identify people who use science, including professionally, in their area and describe how they use science.

Then direct learners to the instructions in the Learner's Book for making and testing their own convex lens.

After they have completed the activity, learners should answer questions 1–3.

In question 3 they can practise the objective: Ask scientific questions and select appropriate scientific enquiries to use. As you walk around the class see what they have decided to test. Encourage them to think up different questions and test them.

> **Practical guidance:** Once again, this is an excellent opportunity for learners to work in pairs or small groups to do the activity themselves – it is simple to do and there are very few resources needed.

> **Differentiation ideas:** Some learners will be less confident to try out their own ideas, but with encouragement from a partner or group member this can be overcome.

> **Assessment ideas:** Have a class discussion about the answers, especially question 3 so that you can combine everybody's ideas for scientific questions.

3 Concave lenses (15 minutes)

Learning intention: Describe how a ray of light changes direction when it travels through different mediums and know that this is called refraction.

Use diagrams to show how light refracts.

Use secondary information sources to find answers to questions.

Resources: A flashlight

Description: This activity does not appear in the Learner's Book.

Show learners this diagram of the concave lens.

Compare it with the diagram of the convex lens in the Learner's Book.

The concave lens causes the light to diverge (spread out). Look at the beam of the flashlight – this uses a concave lens to give a wider beam of light.

Concave lenses are used for spectacles or contact lenses for people who are short-sighted (this means they can see close things but not far away things).

Again, this is a good example of Science in Context 6SIC.04 Identify people who use science, including professionally, in their area and describe how they use science.

Tell learners to draw a diagram of light passing through a concave lens and diverging.

Answers

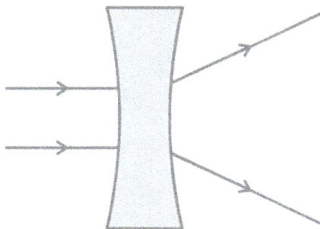

> **Differentiation ideas:** All learners should be able to draw this diagram. You can give them a hint by telling them to think about how the light beams out of a flashlight.

> **Assessment ideas:** Ask a learner to volunteer to draw their diagram on the board. Learners can compare their diagrams with this.

Plenary ideas

1 New words (5–10 minutes)

Resources: Make cards for the new words in this Topic: refraction, medium, optical illusion, lens, convex, converge, focal point

Make two cards for each word so that you have two sets.

Description: Divide the class into two teams. Give a set of cards to each team.

Call out the meanings of the words (see the Language support section at the beginning of this topic for help with this).

The first team to hold up the card matching the description gets a point.

> **Assessment ideas:** The team with the highest score wins.

If there are any words that learners did not recognise, explain these again.

2 Workbook 6.2: Focus exercise (5–10 minutes)

Resources: Workbook

Description: This is a straightforward consolidation exercise on refraction which all learners can do.

Learners write their answers in their workbooks.

> **Assessment ideas:** Learners can take it in turns to call out their answers in class.

CROSS-CURRICULAR LINKS

Working with angles can be linked to Mathematics.

Homework ideas

1   Learners can complete the Workbook exercises– see the description above in Plenary idea 2 for details on the Focus exercise.

The Practice exercise is where learners have to complete a drawing to show how refraction has occurred.

The Challenge exercise is suitable for learners who need a more challenging task. It is based on a photograph of a mirage and learners need to use the internet to find out how refraction causes mirages to happen.

Make sure you go through the answers in your next lesson so that learners can check their work. Or you can take their Workbooks in to mark them.

2 Ask learners to find something at home that uses a convex lens. They must:

a make a drawing or take a photograph of the object

b label the lens

c describe how the lens makes the object useful to us.

You can display learners' work in the classroom.

6.3 The solar system

LEARNING PLAN

Learning objectives	Learning intention	Success criteria
6ESs.01 Describe the relative position and movement of the planets, the Moon and the Sun in the solar system.	• Describe the relative position and movement of the planets, the Moon and the Sun in the solar system.	• Learners can describe the relative position and movement of the planets, the Moon and the Sun in the solar system.
6ESs.02 Observe and describe the changes in the appearance of the Moon over its monthly cycle.	• Observe and describe the changes in the appearance of the Moon over its monthly cycle.	• Learners can observe and describe the changes in the appearance of the Moon over its monthly cycle.
6TWSm.02 Use models, including diagrams, to represent and describe scientific phenomena and ideas.	• Use models, including diagrams, to represent and describe the solar system and the phases of the Moon.	• Learners can use models, including diagrams, to represent and describe the solar system and the phases of the Moon.
6TWSc.05 Take appropriately accurate measurements.	• Take appropriately accurate measurements.	• Learners can take appropriately accurate measurements.
6TWSp.02 Know the features of the five main types of scientific enquiry.	• Practise the science enquiry skills of research, observation over time and pattern seeking.	• Learners can practise research, observation over time and pattern seeking.
6TWSc.07 Use a range of secondary information sources to research and select relevant evidence to answer questions.	• Use a range of secondary information sources to research and answer questions.	• Learners can use a range of secondary information sources to research and answer questions.
6TWSc.08 Collect and record observations and/or measurements in tables and diagrams appropriate to the type of scientific enquiry.	• Collect and record observations in a table.	• Learners can collect and record observations in a table.
6TWSa.05 Present and interpret results using tables, bar charts, dot plots, line graphs and scatter graphs.	• Describe patterns in results, including identifying any results that do not fit the pattern.	• Learners can describe patterns in results, including identifying any results that do not fit the pattern.
6TWSa.02 Describe patterns in results, including identifying any anomalous results.	• Describe patterns in results, including identifying any results that do not fit the pattern.	• Learners can describe patterns in results, including identifying any results that do not fit the pattern.

LANGUAGE SUPPORT

Learners will use the following key words in the topic:

Earth day: a time period of 24 hours

Earth hour: a time period of 60 minutes

Earth year: a time period of $365\frac{1}{4}$ days

phase: in this unit we use this word to describe the changing shapes of the Moon that we can see in its monthly cycle. In everyday English the word 'phase' means a stage or period of time. For example, you are in stage or phase 6 at school

waxing: the increasing in size of the lit up part of the Moon in its monthly cycle. Another meaning of the word 'wax' is the yellow substance made by bees

waning: the decreasing in size of the lit up part of the Moon in its monthly cycle

---

Common misconceptions

Misconception	How to identify	How to overcome
The Moon is only in the sky at night.	Starter idea 2 – If learners answer 'no' to the question, they have the misconception.	Show learners the Moon in the sky in the daytime.

Starter ideas

1 Getting started (5 minutes)

Resources: Learner's Book

Description: This activity will check that learners remember what they learnt about the solar system in earlier stages. Ask questions 1–4 in class.

2 Find the Moon in the sky (15 minutes)

Resources: The Moon in the sky

Description: This activity should help learners overcome the misconception. Check before class that you *can* see the Moon in the sky – it may be a cloudy day so the clouds are covering the Moon up. Also the Moon rises and sets in a different place every day of the month so you will have to search for it. The Moon looks pale during the day because of the bright sunlight, but it *is* always there!

Ask learners: *If we go outside now will we be able to see the Moon?* If learners answer 'No, the Moon is only there at night', then they have the misconception.

Then take them outside and show them the Moon.

Main teaching ideas

1 Think like a scientist 1: Make a scale model of the solar system (60 minutes)

Learning intention: Describe the relative position and movement of the planets, the Moon and the Sun in the solar system.

Use models, including diagrams, to represent and describe the solar system.

Resources: Learner's Book

A tennis or cricket ball, grains of sugar, two peas, two lentils, a long tape measure, nine sticks or poles to push into the ground, paper and a marker pen to make signs, sticky tape, measuring tape; Digital Classroom video: Planets in the solar system (optional)

Description: Begin by looking at the picture of the solar system. If possible, project it onto a screen. Point out the Sun. Point out the four small planets closest to the Sun and the four much bigger planets further away.

Ask learners to name the planets (Mercury, Venus, Earth, Mars, Jupiter, Saturn, Uranus, Neptune).

> **Digital Classroom:** If you have access to the Digital Classroom component, show the video 'Planets in the solar system' at this point. The i button will explain how to use the video.

Talk about the huge distances between objects in the solar system. Read out some of the examples given under the heading Positions of the Sun and planets in the solar system.

Then, to give learners some idea of the scale of objects in the solar system, they should complete Think like a scientist 1: Make a scale model of the solar system.

When they have completed the activity, learners should answer the questions in their notebooks back in the classroom.

> **Practical guidance:** You must select a suitable place to do this activity ahead of time. You need a space at least 250 m long – such as a sports field or open space. Or you could use 150 m and tell learners that planet Neptune is another 100 m beyond Uranus.

They can measure the distances with a tape measure or with paces. One long adult's pace is approximately 1 m. This is an example of using a non-standard measurement (a pace) in place of a standard measurement (metres). The pacing or measuring with a tape measure will be 'appropriately accurate', as worded in objective 6TWSc.05.

If it is not possible to do this activity outside, perhaps you could find a long corridor in the school.

Show the learners the table in the Learner's Book so that they can see the comparative sizes of the Sun and planets in mm and how far apart they are.

Get learners to make the signs before you go outside.

Then go to where you are going to set the model up and carry out steps 2 and 3.

> **Differentiation ideas:** This activity is suitable for all learners.

> **Assessment ideas:** Compare everybody's answers once they have finished.

2   Activity 1: The planets (40 minutes)

Learning intention: Describe the relative positions and movements of the planets, the Moon and the Sun in the solar system.

Use models, including diagrams, to represent and describe the solar system.

Resources: Learner's Book

Description: Revise the two Earth movements and look at the diagrams under Movements of the planets in the solar system.

Tell learners that all the bodies in the solar system make these movements, but that they take different times. Talk about Earth years, Earth days and Earth hours.

Divide the class into teams of about six learners. Try to have a mixture of abilities in each team.

Tell the teams they can refer to the diagram of the solar system and all the information about each planet to answer the questions.

Each team must list their answers on a sheet of paper. Give them a time limit of 5 minutes. As soon as they have finished they must bring their paper to you to check their answers. Note the time for each team.

The team with the most correct answers wins.

> **Differentiation ideas:** Make sure there is a mixture of abilities in each team.

> **Assessment ideas:** The team with the most correct answers wins the quiz. Have a small prize for the winning team.

3   Compare the planets Earth, Mars and Jupiter (30 minutes)

Learning intention: Describe the relative positions and movements of the planets, the Moon and the Sun in the solar system.

Use models, including diagrams, to represent and describe the solar system.

Collect and record observations in a table.

Resources: Workbook Challenge Exercise

Description: This exercise gives a description of the planets Mars and Jupiter. Learners must read the information and compare these planets with Earth by entering answers in a table. They also identify a pattern in the length of orbits and think about the possibilities of life on other planets.

> **Differentiation ideas:** Question 5a is suitable for all learners – they must fill in answers on a table. Questions 5b–5e require learners to think about patterns and reasons for facts about the planets in the text and write their answers in sentences. Question 6 needs learners to use reference sources to find their answers.

> **Assessment ideas:** Ask learners to present their answers in class. Learners can mark their own work.

4   Think like a scientist 2: Observe and describe the phases of the Moon (60 minutes plus the time taken by learners during the month to observe the phases of the Moon)

Learning intention: Observe and describe the changes in the appearance of the Moon over its monthly cycle.

Use models, including diagrams, to represent and describe the solar system.

Practise observation over time and pattern seeking.

Describe patterns in results, including identifying any results that do not fit the pattern.

Use a range of secondary information sources to research and answer questions.

Collect and record observations in a table.

Resources: Learner's Book

Pictures of phases of the Moon

Description: Talk about what the Moon looks like at night. Look at the picture of the full Moon at the beginning of the topic.

Ask:

How is the Moon lit up? (It is lit up by the Sun.)

Is the Moon we see always the same shape? (No, we see everything from a full circle of the Moon to no Moon at all).

Spend some time reading through the information under 'Earth's Moon' and looking at the diagram of the phases of the Moon. If possible, project the diagram on to a screen. Point out the Sun's rays coming in.

Show the half of the Earth facing the Sun lit up and the half of the Moon in all its positions lit up.

Remember that we only see the Moon lit up at night (although the Moon is there in the daytime as well). So imagine you are on the dark half of Earth. Look at each Moon and see what lit up shape you can see.

Talk about the names of each phase. Ask learners how important the crescent Moon is for some countries, such as Malaysia, who have a crescent Moon on their flag.

Introduce the terms 'waxing' and 'waning'.

Learners should then follow the steps in the activity to plan and complete their investigation.

> **Practical guidance:** This is a very important investigation that every learner must do. It will be an opportunity for them to see for themselves what they have been learning about and it will allow them to practise all the learning intentions.

They should begin by making a table with squares for all the days for a month (a calendar). They can draw the shape of the lit up part of the Moon that they can see in the square for each night.

One problem they will have is to find the Moon every night – it will be in a different part of the sky every night. Also, the Moon rises and sets at different times, and some nights may be overcast so

they will not be able to see the Moon at all. So, it is important to explain clearly to learners that you do not expect to see a chart with every single square with a picture of the Moon. Some squares will have a picture of a cloud or heavy rain.

Encourage learners to get family members involved with the activity.

> **Differentiation ideas:** This practical activity is suitable for all learners.

Some learners will find the explanation of why the Moon changes shape difficult. But the more you revisit it, the more likely they will understand. The Workbook has three more exercises where learners have to identify and explain phases.

> **Assessment ideas:** You should take in Learner's Phases of the Moon charts to mark. Set a date 30 days from when they start to take in their work.

Then you can display their charts in class.

Plenary ideas

1 Phase model (10 minutes)

Resources: Worksheet 6.3

Description: Learners make a phase model using the instructions on Worksheet 6.3 and bring it to class. Demonstrate how the model works. Turn the wheel, stopping at different phases and asking learners to identify them.

Ask them to say whether the Moon is waxing or waning between consecutive phases.

> **Assessment ideas:** If learners get an answer wrong, go back to the phases diagram in the Learner's Book to recap the phases of the Moon.

> **Reflection ideas:** How does the model help you to see the different shapes of the Moon?

2 Workbook 6.3: Focus exercise (10–15 minutes)

Resources: Workbook

Description: Learners can consolidate the topic by filling in diagrams of the solar system and the phases of the Moon.

> **Assessment ideas:** You can take in their Workbooks to mark or you can go through answers in class and learners can mark their own work.

CROSS-CURRICULAR LINKS

Working on distances and scale is linked to Mathematics.

Homework ideas

1 Ongoing homework is for learners to look at the Moon each night for their investigation into the phases of the Moon in Think like a scientist 2: Observe and describe the phases of the Moon.

2 Workbook 6.3 Practice exercise. This is a very good exercise for consolidating the topic where learners complete diagrams of the solar system and the phases of the Moon.

3 Research the Moon. Learners can use the internet to find out the most recent things scientists have discovered about the Moon and bring their information to class.

Topic Worksheets

Worksheet 6.3: Make a model of the Moon's phases

Worksheet 6.3 supplies two templates for learners to cut out and make their own phase model by following simple instructions in the worksheet. The model is an excellent way for learners to understand the phases of the Moon.

PROJECT: USING THE MOON'S CYCLE TO MAKE A CALENDAR

6SIC.02 Describe how science is used in their local area.

6SIC.04 Identify people who use science, including professionally, in their area and describe how they use science.

Discuss the topic for the Project with the class. Learners can work in pairs, in small groups or on their own, whichever is most appropriate. Once learners have chosen the religion they want to research they must find information from friends, family, religious leaders and/or the internet. Then they can collect information and pictures and arrange these on an A4 sheet of paper.

Here are some examples of relevant information about Islam, Judaism and Christianity:

The Muslim community uses a lunar calendar. The Moon takes between 29 and 30 days to revolve once around the Earth, so there are 29 or 30 days in each Muslim month. The prophet Mohammed started his calendar or the era of the Hegira in 622 CE. CE means Common Era and BCE means Before Common Era. These terms are the same as AD and BC in the Christian calendar.

The names of the Muslim months are Shawwall, Thul-qada, Thil-giija, Muharram, Safar, Rabil awwal, Rabi-ul-thani, Jamdil-ula, Jamdith thani, Rajab, Shabaan and Ramadaan.

For Muslims all over the world, the month of Ramadaan is very important. It is a time for spiritual rejuvenation. Ramadaan is the ninth month of the Islamic lunar calendar and one of the five pillars of Islam.

The Jewish calendar uses the Moon for counting the days of the month. The starting point of their calendar is the biblical creation of the world, which happened in 3761 BCE.

In the Jewish community, the holy or Sabbath day lasts from sunset on Friday night to sunset on Saturday night. Jewish families celebrate with a special Sabbath meal on Friday nights.

The Moon also plays a part in the Christian calendar. Easter Sunday is the first Sunday after the full Moon which occurs on or after March 21. If the full Moon occurs on a Sunday, Easter day is the following Sunday.

Give learners a week or two before they have to hand in their project.

Display the projects in the classroom.

Learners can assess each other's work using questions such as these:

* How eye-catching is the project?
* How interesting is the information?
* Are the pictures relevant and interesting?

Assessment rubric

Here are some guidelines for assessment:

How well did the learner...	Very well	Adequately	Not much effort made
find relevant information?			
present the information, including pictures and/or photographs?			
arrange all the information on an A4 page?			

> Glossary

accumulate – to increase over time. For example, the runner accumulated a big collection of medals over the years

accurate – correct and true, more real, without mistakes

angle: the space between two lines that meet at a surface, measured in degrees

artificial fertiliser – a fertiliser is a mixture of organic matter and minerals that help plants to grow. An artificial fertiliser is a factory-made fertiliser made from chemicals

astronaut – a person who goes into space

barrier – an object that stops things getting through or past it

blood – a red liquid that carries food and oxygen to all parts of the body

blood vessels – special tubes that carry the blood around the body

boiling point – the temperature at which particles throughout a liquid become a gas

breathing – the way we take air into our lungs and let it out again

breathing rate – the number of times we breathe in and out in one minute

burial – burying of sediments with many layers of sediments above

carbon dioxide – a waste gas that the body must get rid of

cast – a fossil where the bones of the whole animal are preserved in minerals

circuit diagram – a diagram of a circuit using conventional symbols for all the components

circulation – the pumping of blood all around the body

circulatory system – the system formed by the heart, blood vessels and blood to carry food and oxygen around the body

composition – what something is made or consists of

compost – a natural fertiliser made of dead organic matter such as dead leaves and insects

conduction – the transfer of heat energy from one object to another

conventional symbol – a symbol that is recognised all over the world

converge – to meet or come together

convex – a bulging shape

crystal – the particular shaped structure of a mineral

crystalline – the adjective for crystal

defence – protection against something

deposit – to put down or drop

diaphragm – a muscle in the chest that helps us to breathe in and out

displaced – the moving aside of water as a result of upthrust

earth day – a time period of 24 hours

earth hour – a time period of 60 minutes

earth year – a time period of 365¼ days

electrical conductors – materials and substances that conduct electricity well

environment – the air, water, land and living things around us

erode – to wear down weathered rocks into sediments

evidence – the things we know that show us that something has happened or changed

extrusive igneous rock – an igneous rock that has formed from lava cooling down on the surface of the Earth

fertilisation – the joining of a male sex cell and a female sex cell

focal point – the point where rays of light converge

food chain: a drawing that shows the order in which animals eat plants and other animals to get energy

food web – a number of linked food chains

forcemeter – a device to weigh objects in newtons (N)

fossil – the preserved remains of animals and plants in sedimentary rocks

geologist – a scientist who studies rocks

gneiss – metamorphic rock made from granite. This word is pronounced the same as 'nice'

heart – the special muscle that pumps blood around the body

hormones – chemicals in the body that cause the body changes that happen during puberty

host – the living thing that a parasite infects

hygiene – keeping yourself and the things around you clean

igneous rock – a rock which comes from magma that has cooled down into solid rock

incident ray – the ray of light that arrives at the mirror

intrusive igneous rock – an igneous rock that has formed when magma cools down inside the Earth's crust

irreversible – cannot be changed back to the way it was before

lens – a transparent material such as glass, Perspex or plastic with at least one curved surface

loam – a soil with a balance of sand, clay and organic matter

lungs – the organs we use for breathing

mass – a large intrusion of igneous rock

mass – the quantity of matter in an object. Mass is measured in kilograms (kg)

medium – a material such as air, water or glass

melting point – the temperature at which a solid becomes a liquid

menstruation – a period of bleeding caused by the release of the womb lining and an unfertillized egg, which occurs once a month

metamorphic rock – a rock that has been changed by heat or pressure or both heat and pressure

microplastics – very small particles of plastic that make their way into the environment, especially rivers and seas

mineral – part of a rock made of different substances with a crystal structure

mirror image – reflection in a mirror

mould – a fossil which makes an impression in rock of exactly the same shape and size as the animal or plant

mucus – a sticky substance found in our noses, windpipe and other air passages

naked eye – we can see something with our eyes without the help of a magnifying glass or hand lens

newton – the unit of measure for weight, named after Isaac Newton who explained the force of gravity

normal: a line drawn at right angles (90°) to the surface of the mirror

nutrients: food in the form of organic matter and minerals such as iron and phosphates

optical illusion – something our eyes see but it is not real

organic matter – living things or things which were alive, such as dead leaves, bits of root and twigs

ova – female sex cells

oxygen – a gas in the air that the body uses

parallel circuit – a circuit where there is more than one pathway and each pathway receives the full circuit voltage

parasite – any living thing that lives on or in the body of another living thing

periscope – a device that uses mirrors for you to see things otherwise out of sight

pesticide – a factory-made product that kills unwanted insects but also kills the organic matter in the soil

phase – the changing shapes of the Moon in its monthly cycle

physical change – any change that does not change a substance into a different substance

plane mirror – a flat mirror, rather than a mirror with a curved surface such as a concave or convex mirror

preserved – means kept forever

pressure – the force that is exerted on or against an object by something in contact with it

products – the new substances that form in a chemical reaction

property – something about a substance that allows us to tell it apart from other substances

puberty – the age at which a person becomes able to reproduce

pulse – a small beat felt under the skin due to the pressure of blood as the heart pumps it around the body

rate – how fast something happens

react – to interact and change to make a new substance; also to respond to something

reactants – the substances that react together in a chemical reaction reflected ray: the ray of light that reflects off the mirror

refract/refraction – the bending of light

rehabilitation – to restore your body to health

repellent – a substance that keeps insects away

represent – to show or stand for; for example, the colour red usually represents danger

reproductive system – the parts of the body that make the sex cells

reversible – can be changed back to the way it was before

sediment – very small pieces of rock

sedimentary rock – a rock made from small pieces of other rock stuck together

sedimentation – the process where sediments build up in layers on the sea bed or lake bed

series circuit – a circuit where the electric current only has one pathway

soil – a mixture of broken up rocks, organic matter, water and air

solidification – the process where liquid magma or lava cools down and becomes solid rock

solute – he solid in a solution

solvent – the liquid in a solution

sperm – male sex cells

symbol – small sign used on a diagram to represent a real thing; for example, the symbol ✓ means 'correct' and the symbol ✗ means 'wrong'

texture – the feel of a material; for example, rough or smooth

thermal conductors – materials and substances that conduct heat well

toxic – harmful or poisonous; for example, the factory produced toxic gases

transport – to carry

uniform – the same throughout

upthrust – a force that pushes up to an object in water or air

valley – the landform that a river erodes in the rocks. The river flows in the valley

vectors – living things that spread diseases but do not get the diseases themselves

volt (V) – the unit for measuring strength of electricity

voltage – the strength of electricity needed for an electrical component or appliance to work

waning Moon – the decreasing in size of the lit-up part of the Moon in its monthly cycle

waterlogged – full of water that will not drain through

waxing Moon – the increasing in size of the lit-up part of the Moon in its monthly cycle

weathering – a process where heat, ice, rain or plant roots break up rocks

weight – the force of attraction on an object caused by gravity. Weight is measured in newtons (N)

weightlessness – a state of having no weight because there is no gravity

windpipe – he air tube that carries air from the nose and mouth to the lungs and back again